GENERATIVE GRAMMAR
(CHOMSKYAN OR UNIVERSAL)

AN INTRODUCTORY HANDBOOK

M.M. SASI

INDIA • SINGAPORE • MALAYSIA

ISBN

Hardcase 979-8-89777-875-1
Paperback 979-8-89744-291-1

Cover design: **M. S. Syam Leneesh**

Other works from the author

MONTESSORI – A BRIEF GUIDE

Montessori: A Brief Guide is an insightful book that delves into the life and work of Dr. Maria Montessori, highlighting her revolutionary contributions to education and child psychology. It offers an in-depth exploration of her innovative educational methodology and philosophy, emphasising the use of Montessori materials and providing practical guidance on how to handle them effectively. Designed as a training guide for teachers, the book also serves as a valuable resource for parents, offering practical advice for fostering a child's holistic development. It discusses the groundbreaking ideas Dr. Montessori introduced, which transformed the world's understanding of a child's potential. Her dedication to uncovering and nurturing the hidden capacities of children marked her as a pioneer in child-focused education, making this guide an essential tool for educators and parents alike.

To,

My grandchildren, Aliakya Syam, Anagh Syam, Abhayroop Syam, Dakshina Syam, and Vihana Syam, inspire me to be young enough to walk ahead.

CONTENTS

PREFACE

Noam Chomsky dropped a grammar bomb in 1957, namely Syntactic structures whose effects radiated to the realm of all worldwide languages. The great grammarians and linguists of the day became dumbstruck; many began to reconstruct while others started building fortresses around themselves to defend their artifices' old versions.

The most sought-after legendary genius, who was then famous as a political commentator, mathematician, and columnist, surprised everyone in his new incarnation as a linguist and grammar writer. Although he declared it merely a hereditary achievement, the world watched him with disbelief as he busted many myths about language.

Chomsky consolidates the hypotheses of Dr. Montessori and Sigmund Freud that language acquisition is an inherent quality of the human child and occurs in the most profound consciousness of his mind. Contrary to what people think, many linguists argue that a language can never be taught. The most embarrassing part of his revelation was that most languages, regardless of their origin of time and place, have a universal structure. And so, he called his grammar Universal Grammar (UG).

Long before him, Descartes initiated the descriptive path in the study of philosophy, separating himself from the prescriptive methodology, the order of the day. Chomsky argued that the time has come to adapt the descriptive method in the study of linguistics, too, as it reflects reality.

The descriptive and prescriptive methods offer contrasting approaches to analysing scientific subjects. This approach is concerned with observing, documenting and explaining natural occurrences with the goal of providing an objective account of the facts found where no additional action is taken. It focuses on recognising and interpreting patterns rather than imposing preconceived rules or judgments. The prescriptive approach, on the other hand, aims to set norms, guidelines, or standards as per a theoretical framework or an intended outcome. It wants to outline what ought to be rather than what is.

The grammatical aspect of language is concerned; the descriptive approach is that a language must be studied, understood, and analysed as it is used, regardless of standards, by its native speakers. While the prescriptive method specifies, insists upon, or guides the use of language otherwise, it may not consider certain varieties to be the same language. For example, ghetto dialects are far from the analysis of linguists belonging to the prescriptivists; the elite array is the only language to them. A further impossibility of prescriptive grammar is that the laws of language belong to the class of the laws of nature and, therefore, cannot be prescriptive. For instance, we can observe and describe how a tree grows, but we cannot prescribe how it should develop.

Generative Grammar, the descriptive methodology developed by Noam Chomsky, has revolutionised the study of linguistics and is widely accepted, if not compellingly so, by scholars and researchers around the world. The descriptive method, which involves observing and describing phenomena as they are, is an attempt to provide a factually accurate account without bias. The focus of the curriculum is to learn and analyse more about the patterns rather than utilising rules to understand those patterns better—theories. It sets out to prescribe how things ought to be instead of describing how they are.

Regardless of the names of languages, grammar is not static, which means that humanity goes ahead to change languages, originate new ones, or even perish. However, according to this version of grammar, even if the language changes, there will be a structure that can be identified as a characteristic common to all languages. This discovery makes generative grammar such a big deal.

Generative grammar, whose early development involved scholars like Noam Chomsky, has met with both widespread acceptance and considerable criticism over the decades. Chomsky's methods resulted in interpretation and reformulation. Still, even if his approach has left its mark on theories of linguistics and many linguistic forms (chaos linguistics), there is no consensus among the scholars. And yet, it is worth pointing out that no linguist today completely denies the fundamental tenets of generative grammar, reflecting its lasting significance. However, there is now an even more critical need to bring these discussions to educators, teachers, and others interested in more practical languages, with an in-the-classroom-strategy focus rather than a philosophical one.

This book aims to demystify generative grammar and introduce its concepts to a broader audience. Its aim is not to settle academic debates but to make the principles of this influential approach more approachable and relevant to those engaged in teaching and understanding language. Once this goal is achieved, the mission of this book will be fulfilled.

For many years, I have been teaching English, relying on traditional grammar to explain linguistic concepts to my students. However, I often found myself unable to address specific complex grammatical problems adequately. It was during the 2000s, when internet access became more widespread, that I stumbled upon the revolutionary ideas of Noam Chomsky on generative grammar. Curiosity compelled me to dive deep into the subject, studying Universal Grammar theories, principles, and best practices. It was a whole new level of appreciation, above and beyond traditional grammar, that left me inspired in this whole new way.

I discovered, while learning about the subject, that even though there were many advanced materials regarding it, there was a considerable gap when it came to more introductory literature regarding those ideas. A small but comprehensive book could serve this purpose, I realised, and make Chomskyan grammar accessible to a larger audience. This gave rise to the idea that I am working on a challenging but worthwhile effort to write this book. So, I set myself this very hard of a task, and here it is: Generative Grammar (Chomskyan or Universal), an effort of necessity and passion, time-consuming but fruitful work, a book designed to serve as a handy, user-friendly introduction to this exciting field.

If you are a teacher, this will bring much dynamism to your class. You will get plenty of clarity in your language if you are a creative author. And finally, if you are a linguistics student, this will undoubtedly change how you handle it.

– M.M. Sasi
25-01-2025

INTRODUCTION

Let us begin with the question: what is a language? A language is a set of sentences whose number of sentences stands for infinitive. If I explain this point further, the corpus of sentences has two aspects. To say that the producer of sentences and the recipient can construct and understand an infinite number of sentences. These are the two sides of the same piece, which means one cannot exist alone: therefore, the two co-occurred. And, of course, these two elements form an integral part of linguistic acquisition. In conclusion, it is essential to emphasise that sentences should also be legitimate. That is to say, a language is a set of infinitive and legitimate sentences.

Then, thc question arises: What is grammar?

Grammar is the mechanism by which legitimate sentences are constructed and understood in every language. If I develop this point further, we can say that grammar is a finite set of rules or principles that systematically generate all the grammatically correct sentences in a language while excluding ungrammatical ones.

In this book, we discuss grammar not because there is a shortage of grammar but because there is something new and unprecedented about Generative Grammar. Noam Chomsky calls it generative in the mathematical sense of the term a+b=c.

If a =3 and b =2, c will be 5

and if a = 4 and b=5, c will be nine and so on.

Likewise, sentences are also generated in a language when values are added. In a general sense, it is the syntax of a language.

We must never forget that syntax is not just a concept but the very essence of language construction. As Chomsky defines it, syntax is the study of the principles and processes that govern how sentences are formed in a specific language. This does not simply concern where words are placed within a phrase but principles that form the core of everything written or spoken. We will explore in depth these tenets, which are the foundation of our understanding of language.

The evolution of generative grammar has occurred through several influential theories and frameworks, most notably based on the innovative publications of Noam Chomsky. It began with the Phrase Structure Grammar (PSG), introduced in his seminal work *Syntactic Structures (1957),* which provided a formal way to describe sentence structure using rewrite rules. This framework was soon expanded into Transformational Generative Grammar (TGG), outlined in *Aspects of the Theory of Syntax (1965).* Chomsky introduced deep and surface structures and transformational rules to account for syntactic variations. By the 1980s, Chomsky proposed the Government and Binding Theory in *Lectures on Government and Binding (1981),* which replaced transformational rules with modular principles like X-bar theory, case theory, and binding theory. In the 1990s, Noam Chomsky proposed the Minimalist Program in *The Minimalist Program* (1995), advocating against an extensive and language-specific architecture of grammar in favour of a more economical and universal account: Syntactic structures are built out of elementary operations such as Merge and Move. This hierarchy represents a streamlining and the ideal explanatory complexity, fusing innate and universal in human language.

Noam Chomsky also splits language into I-language and E-language. The former is an internal language within an individual, and the latter is an abstract form of existence in an individual's outer arena. So, he suggests that I-language is linked to grammar, whereas E-language should be under the purview of linguists. The most exciting aspect of the whole story is that throughout these developments, we will see the main criticisms and rectifications of the theories from the beginning, mainly from Chomsky himself.

Something akin to these statements that you may have understood better is Chomsky's second significant contribution, which is the universality of grammar. All human languages have a standard underlying structure that is managed by innate principles encoded in the human mind. This is a fundamental idea in Noam Chomsky's theory of Universal Grammar (UG), which suggests that the capacity to learn and use language is biologically hard-wired so that humans can produce an infinite number of novel sentences with a set of finite rules.

Despite surface differences in languages, Generative Grammar argues that deeper syntactic and structural similarities exist, such as hierarchical organisation, recursion, and dependency relations. Universal Grammar provides the framework for these shared principles, while language-specific parameters account for variations among languages.

Grammar universality highlights the innate specificity of language as a human trait and supports the intuition that linguistic competence is generated via an identical template for all humans.

Now that we are taking our first steps into the world of Generative Grammar, one thing you should keep very close to your heart is that you, the reader, are the centre of every learning process. In this book, we will discuss everything one needs to know when learning Generative Grammar, and each point will be elaborated with examples so you can understand it correctly. But don't forget that your understanding of these concepts will not be perfect after just one read. You are asked to come to learn and to grow; this means that your active participation is essential.

As stated above, the primary purpose of this book is to provide a summary but thorough explanation of grammar, specifically for readers with an interest in the ideas behind it. This is not work mentored under heavy hitters in academia but the result of some self-space and serious digging. While the author has done everything possible to present each idea clearly and thoroughly, mistakes or misinterpretations of the evidence are inevitable. Consequently, the author apologises and takes full responsibility for any failures and welcomes friendly readers to share constructive criticism and add corrections in later prints. The author has tried their utmost to summarise the concepts as accurately as possible without much training and invites all comments, lending that no flaw shall be identified until a correction follows, writing for the benefit of its readers.

Above all, I am profoundly grateful to my life partner, Annie, whose patience, unwavering encouragement, and wholehearted support through both good and challenging times have been a pillar of strength in accomplishing this task. It is with deep appreciation and humility that I present this work to its readers.

moorikkattilsasi@gmail.com

CHAPTER I

GENERATIVE GRAMMAR

There is a custom way of starting all traditional grammatical texts, defining the sentence as a group of words with a complete meaning, leaving the completeness of meaning to ambiguity. However, one thing is obvious: meaning was what mattered most. We can only talk about Generative Grammar if we entirely set aside the concept.

Noam Chomsky begins his grammar by defining syntax as the study of the principles and processes by which sentences are constructed, leaving meaning to their fate after construction. The prime show will play syntax as the main theme, which means it came to the central stage and is still under the spotlight.

We start by making two diagrams. The first diagram charts traditional linguistics. We will now look at the second diagram, which reflects the linguistic aspects of Generative grammar as a visual tool to understand its diverse characteristics and principles.

The first diagram shows how the term linguistics is understood in terms of traditional grammar.

After this, we will approach linguistics through the lens of Generative grammar.

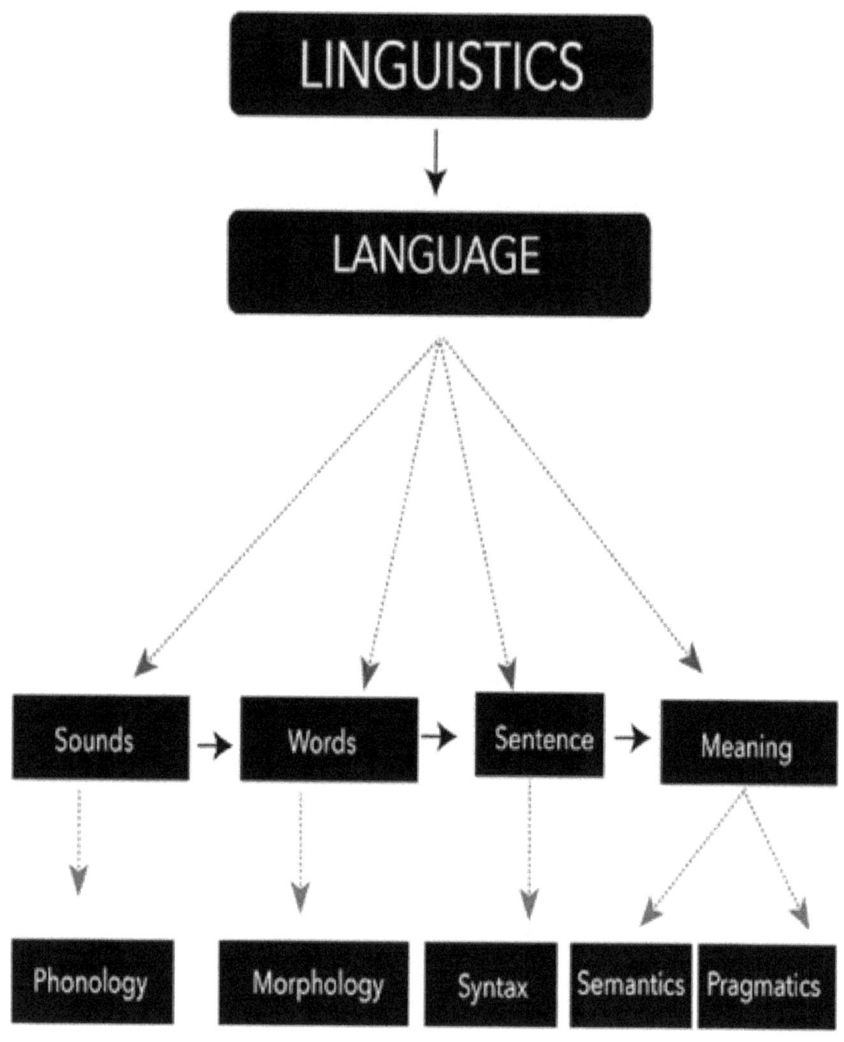

The first diagram illustrates how the term linguistics is interpreted through traditional grammar.

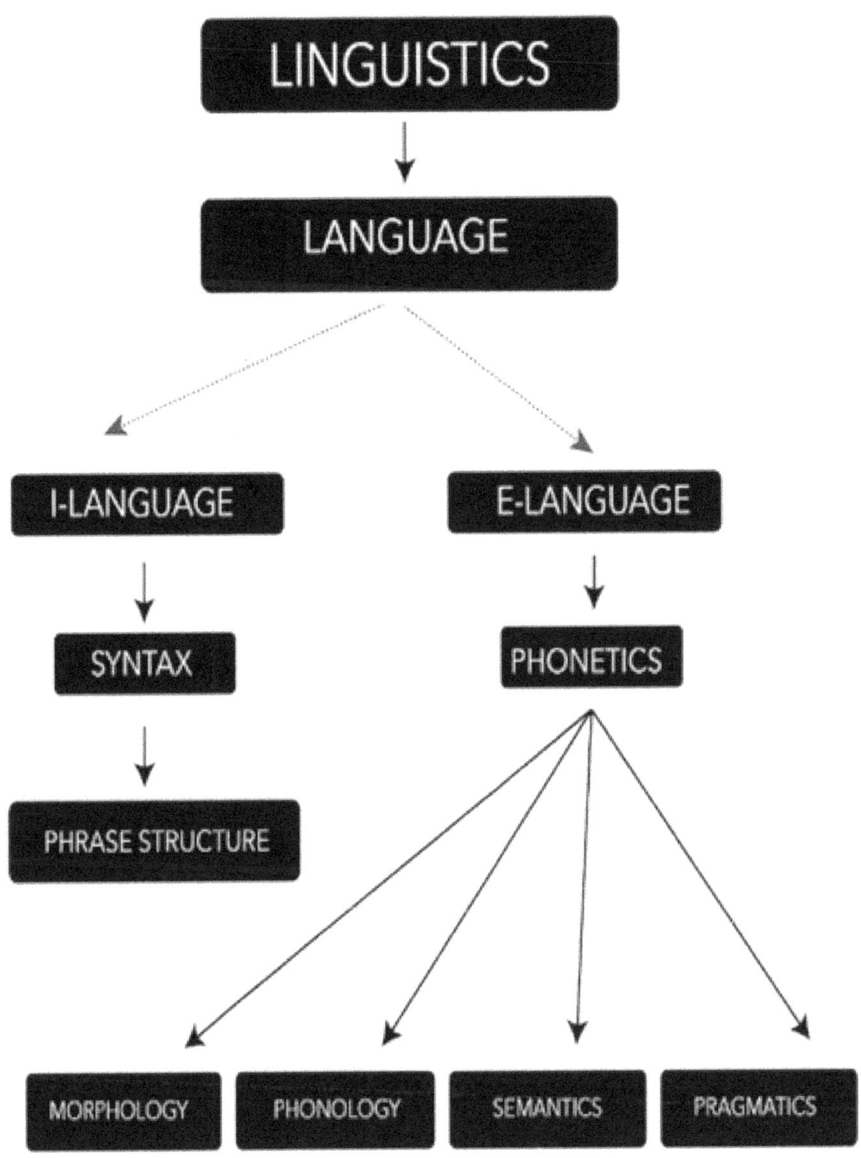

The next one shows the term linguistics from the perspective of Generative grammar.

I-LANGUAGE AND E-LANGUAGE

Noam Chomsky introduced the concepts of I-language and E-language. These concepts serve as a crucial framework for distinguishing two perspectives on studying language:

I-Language (Internal Language):

I-Language is the internalised form of language residing in the mind of a speaker.

- It is a mental, individual, and abstract representation of linguistic competence.
- Represents the generative grammar that produces all possible sentences in a language.
- Concerned with the biological and cognitive processes underlying language.
- It focuses on language as part of the human mind/brain and seeks to understand the principles and structures innate to human cognition.

Example: Studying how a speaker of English understands grammar or forms sentences internally.

E-Language (External Language):

E-language refers to externalised language, i.e., the observable manifestations of language in speech, writing, or social communication.

- It is an external, societal view of language as a collection of utterances, texts, or linguistic behaviours.
- It often focuses on language as a social phenomenon, considering usage, variation, and historical change.

- Associated with behaviourist and descriptive approaches to linguistics.

Example: Analysing the linguistic patterns of a group of English speakers in a community.

According to Generative Grammar (GG) and what the above charts show, syntax makes the whole language first in collaboration with the mind; in other words, the human mind constructs the language syntactically. Thus, syntax becomes the very mechanism of the mind to build and comprehend a language; therefore, the same is the possible way to compute a language. Another thing worth mentioning is that we create unlimited phrases, which form the language with limited resources, meaning, a limited number of signs, sounds and words. However, the human brain constructs I-language in a way that it knows perfectly, and this mechanism is, in generative grammar, called grammar. I-language is notated as an internal language but is sometimes mentioned as intentional language, showing the conscious intervention of the mind to produce sentences. Similarly, the external language is also called extensive language, clarifying that it is expanded for a purpose. However, both cases say that the mind owns the property of constructing the sentences and a specific procedure to generate them. These generative values are known as Phrase Structure Principles.

Phrase Structure Principles

Let us delve into the fundamental principles of phrase structure. These principles are the building blocks of our understanding of generative grammar. While there are derivative extensions to these principles, it is crucial to grasp these fundamentals first. So, let us discuss them step by step, engaging in a committed learning process.

1. S→ NP+VP
2. NP→ T+N
3. VP→ V+NP
4. T→ the
5. N→, man, ball, etc.
6. V→ hit, took etc

A formula is generalised and abstract, and the above equations are the same. The constraint of the mechanism that formulates the above statements is that the human mind unpredictably generates them. In this case, generalisations are necessary because each sentence in a language is not explicitly learned, taught or parsed, as they are infinite in number. To understand the above principles, we must put aside the concept that a sentence is a linear arrangement of words to produce a sense. Instead, it is a set of components, known as phrases, syntactically built to form a more significant component or components to convey specific ideas, thoughts, feelings, emotions, etc.

The first principle says S→NP+VP that a sentence consists of two components: Noun Phrase (NP) and Verb Phrase. (VP)

The second principle systematically outlines the components of a noun phrase: NP→T+N, where T represents the (article), and N stands for Noun. These are the fourth and fifth principles, providing a structured understanding of language structure.

The third principle tells which components form a verb phrase: Verb (V) and Noun Phrase (NP). The sixth statement describes what a verb is like.

If we rewrite the statement S→NP+VP:

1. NP+VP
2. T+N+VP
3. T+N+V+NP
4. The +N +V +NP
5. the + boy +Verb +NP
6. the + boy + hit +NP
7. the + boy + hit+ T+ N
8. the +boy +hit +the +N
9. the +boy +hit +the +ball.

These are the nine steps that take a string to form a sentence that consists of three constituents.

The above boxes show how constituents are formed. "The boy" is a constituent (NP) composed of T and N, and "hit the ball" is another constituent composed of a minor constituent NP embedded in a larger constituent, VP. All three constituents together form the largest constituent, the sentence.

TREE DIAGRAM

In generative grammar, a tree diagram is a visual representation that shows the hierarchical organisation of a sentence, beginning with the top node (the sentence, or "S") and splitting downwards to the terminal nodes (the lexical elements, or words). Unlike a natural tree that grows upward, the syntactic tree diagram "grows" downward, starting with the root node and branching out into the constituent parts of the sentence. These branches reflect how phrases are organised, such as Noun phrases (NP), Verb phrases (VP), and Prepositional phrases (PP), and show how smaller units combine to form larger structures.

Tree diagrams play an important role in generative grammar, as they visually represent sentences and how they are hierarchically constructed. They can also depict complex sentences and help clarify ambiguous ones. A sentence with an abundance of potential interpretations can have its tree diagram exhibited in a way that features the diverse syntactic organisations accountable for each distinct significance.

Now, let's see how a tree diagram interprets the sentence "the boy hit the ball."

The tree diagram explicitly interprets the sentence "The boy hit the ball" and visualises its hierarchical syntactic structure. At the topmost level, the sentence (S) is divided into two main branches: a Noun phrase (NP) representing the subject and a Verb phrase (VP) representing the predicate.

The subject NP is further branched into two components: a determiner (D) and a noun (N). In this example, the determiner (D) is "the", and the noun (N) is "boy". These are the terminal nodes of the subject NP.

The VP, representing the predicate, is similarly broken down into two components: a verb (V) and another NP, which serves as the object. The verb (V) is "hit", and the object NP is further divided into a determiner (D) and a noun (N). In this case, the determiner (D) is "the", and the noun (N) is "ball". These are the terminal nodes of the object NP.

Thus, the tree diagram starts from the highest hierarchical node (S) and branches downward through intermediate syntactic categories (NP, VP, D, N, V) until it reaches the terminal nodes, which are the actual lexical items ("the," "boy," "hit," "the," "ball"). This explicit representation allows us to clearly see how the sentence is constructed and how each word contributes to its overall structure.

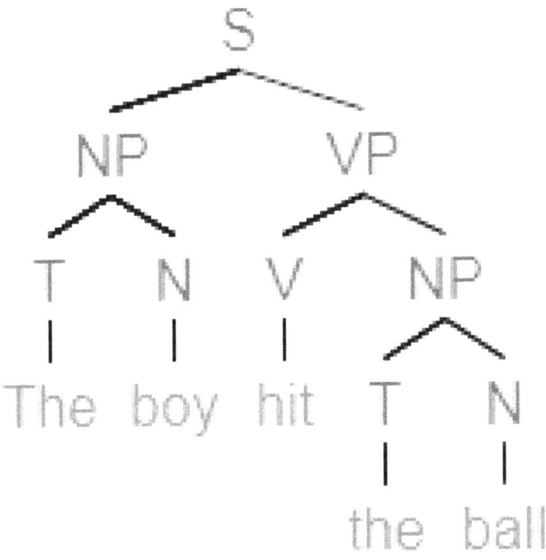

This clarity enhances one's understanding of a sentence's structure.

Here is an example of how a tree diagram maps out the ambiguity of a sentence.

Sentence: The mechanic fixed the car in the garage (ambiguous).

Clarification by tree diagram:

1

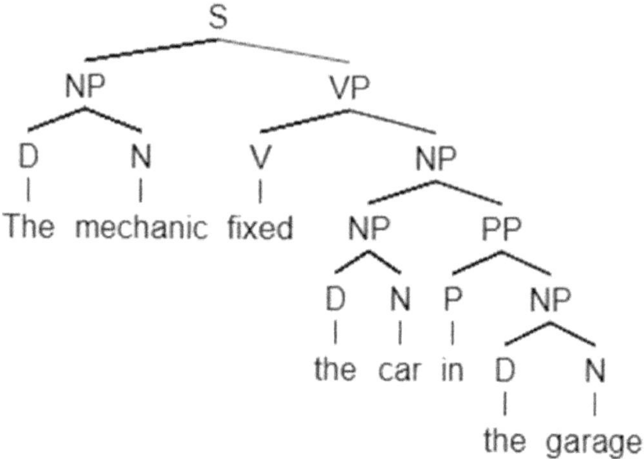

2

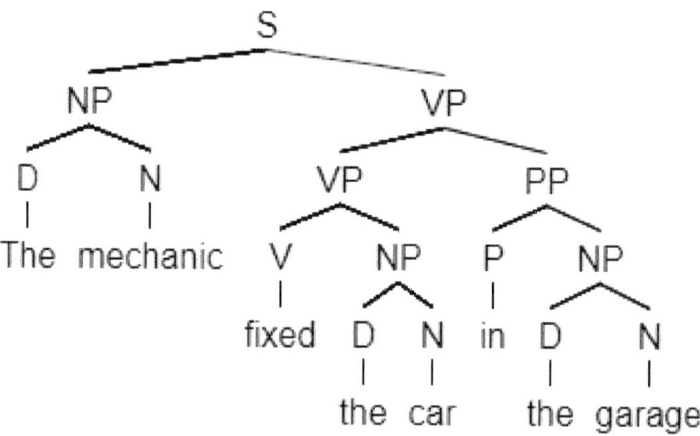

Diagram 1 interprets the meaning of the sentence as the mechanic fixing the car that was in the garage, not parked somewhere else.

Diagram 2 interprets the meaning of the sentence as he did the fixing in the garage.

It is preferable to know how the techniques of connecting a tree diagram's ramifications are known.

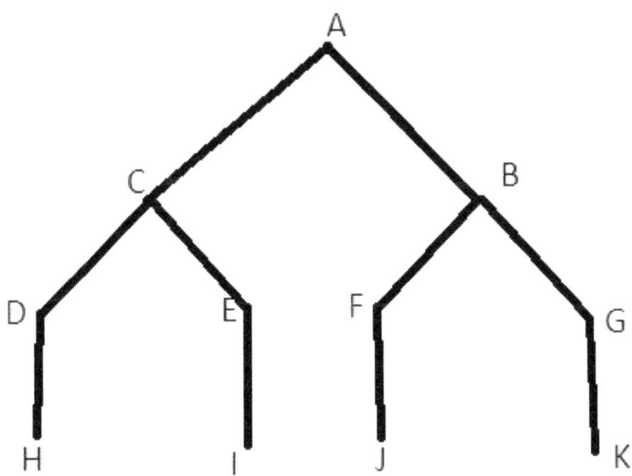

In the diagram, A is the highest hierarchy from which it begins to grow. This means that B and C are daughter nodes of A, while B and C are sister nodes to one another. B and C become mother nodes to produce other sister nodes, D, E, F, and G. It is a never-ending process. In the diagram provided, H, I, J, and K can be mother nodes, but they ultimately become end nodes or terminal nodes without doing so.

Parentheses as alternatives to a tree diagram.

Generative grammar allows for sentences to be represented in a nested, parenthetical format to demonstrate their inherent hierarchy in lieu of a diagrammed tree structure. Within this notation, each constituent of a sentence is enclosed parenthetically to delineate relationships from the inside out. In doing so, the nested parentheses provide a one-dimensional means of depicting structural organisation without requiring the level of visual complexity involved with drawing the complete branching diagram. This parenthetical method succinctly illustrates how constituent parts are interconnected within the greater whole of a sentence.

For example, consider the sentence:

"The boy hit the ball."

Its structure using parentheses can be represented as:

[S [NP [D The] [N boy]] [VP [V hit [NP [D the] [N ball]]]]

Here:

- S represents the sentence.
- The NP (Noun Phrase) for the subject contains a determiner (D) "The" and a noun (N) "boy."
- The VP (Verb Phrase) includes a verb (V), "hit", and another NP for the object, which has a determiner (D) "the" and a noun (N) "ball."

Another example:

"She plays piano beautifully."

[S [NP [N She]] [VP [V plays] [NP [N piano]] [Adv beautifully]]]

This format shows the same hierarchical structure as a tree diagram but in a linear, textual form. While it may lack the visual clarity of a tree diagram, it is concise and practical for compact representation, especially in linguistic texts or discussions.

CONSTITUENTS

Constituents form the building blocks of sentences, linking words into meaningful groups that work together. Whether short or long, simple or complex, constituents of varying types collaborate to convey complete ideas through linguistic structure. We can detect these elemental units and explore their interconnections through strategic questioning and visual maps that depict their places within the orchestrated whole.

Types of Constituents

1. **Noun Phrase (NP):**

A group of words centred around a noun, functioning as the subject, object, or complement.

- The tall boy with glasses (NP)

Tree structure:

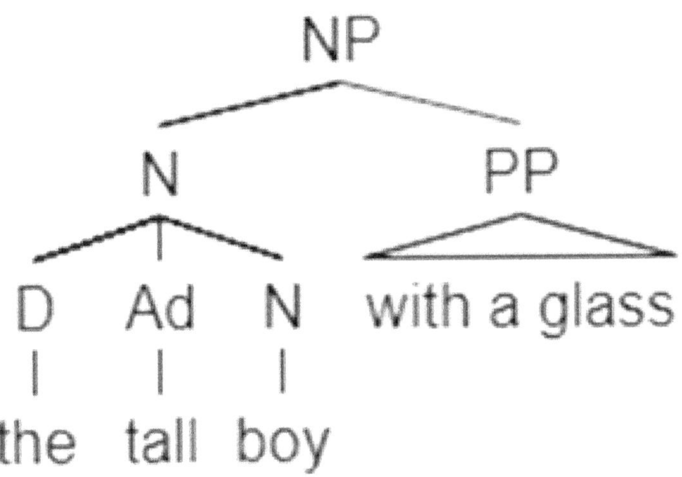

2. **Verb Phrase (VP):**

- A group of words centred around a verb, functioning as the predicate.
- Example.

Ran quickly to the park (VP)

- Tree structure:

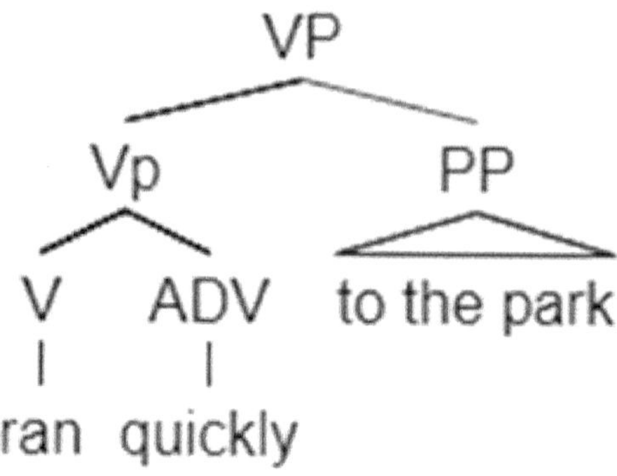

3. Prepositional Phrase (PP):

- A preposition and its complement (often a noun phrase).
- Example:
- Under the table (PP)
- Tree structure.

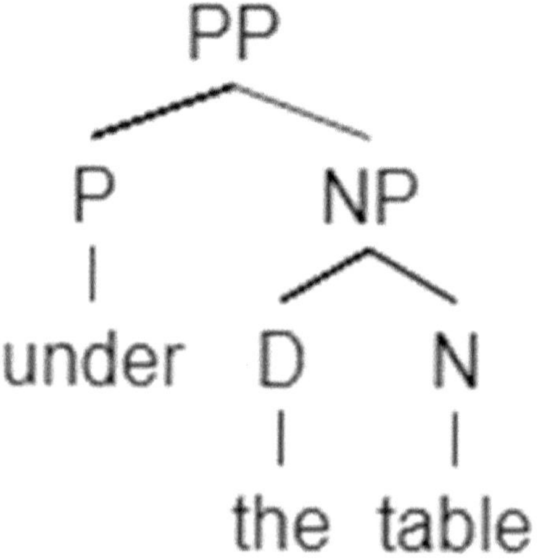

4. Adjective Phrase (AdjP):

- A phrase centred around an adjective.
- Example:
- Very happy about the news (AdjP)
- Tree structure:

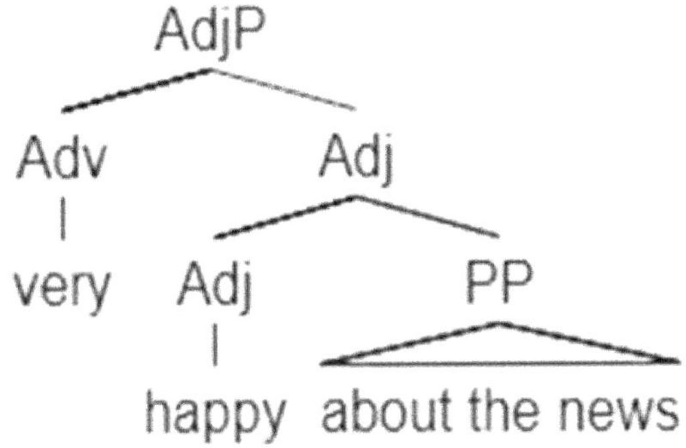

5. Adverb Phrase (AdvP):

- A phrase centred around an adverb.
- Example:
- Quite quickly (AdvP)
- Tree structure:

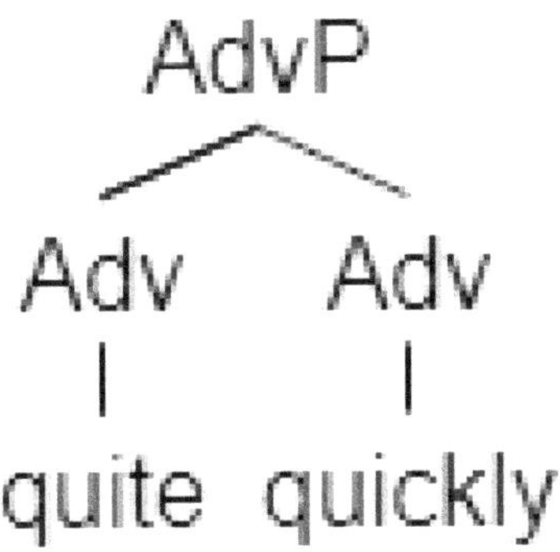

6. Clause (Complementiser Phrase) (CP):

- A group of words containing a subject and a predicate can be independent or dependent.
- Example:
- That she was late (CP)
- Tree structure:

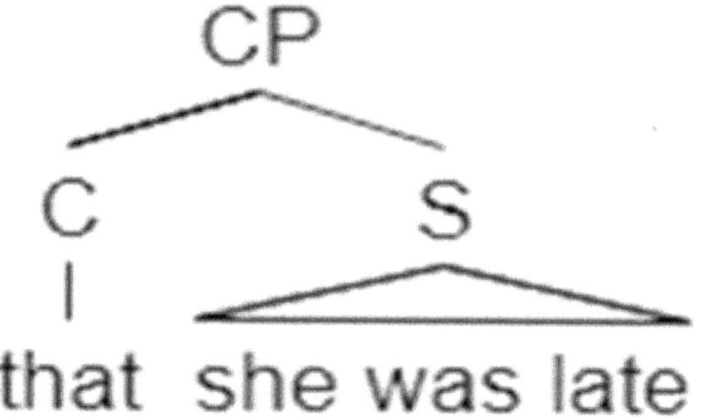

CONSTITUENCY TESTS

To determine whether a group of words forms a constituent, you can use the following tests:

1. **Substitution Test:**

- Replace the group of words with a single word (pronoun, pro-verb, etc.).
- Example:
- Original: The tall boy with glasses ran.
- Substitution: He ran. (The NP, the tall boy with glasses, is replaced by the pronoun he.)
- The phrase the tall boy with glasses is a constituent (NP).

2. Movement Test:

- Move the group of words to a different position in the sentence.
- Example:
- Original: The tall boy with glasses ran to the park.
- Movement: To the park, the tall boy with glasses ran. (The PP to the park moved to the front of the sentence)
- The phrase to the park is a constituent (PP).

3. **Coordination Test:**

- Combine the group with a similar structure using a conjunction.
- Example:
- Original: The tall boy with glasses ran.
- Coordination: The tall boy with glasses and the short girl ran. (the NP, the tall boy with glasses, coordinated with the NP, the short girl)
- The phrase The tall boy with glasses is a constituent (NP).

4. **Ellipsis Test:**

- Remove the group of words in a context where meaning remains clear.
- Example:
- Original: The tall boy ran, and the short girl did, too.
- Ellipsis: 'Did too' implies ran, so the tall boy is a constituent.

Observe the following examples and their Tree Diagrams

Sentence: The boy ran to the park.

Tree Structure:

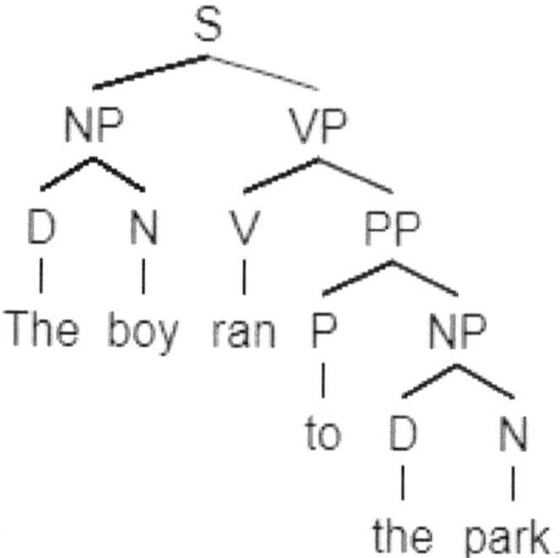

This hierarchical structure shows how the sentence is divided into its constituents: NP (the boy) and VP (ran to the park), with further subdivisions.

Application of Constituency Tests on the Example

1. Substitution:

- Replace 'The boy': He ran to the park. → The boy is a constituent.
- Replace 'to the park': The boy ran there. → As they replaced the whole part of the sentence, 'To the park' is a constituent.

Tree Diagram:

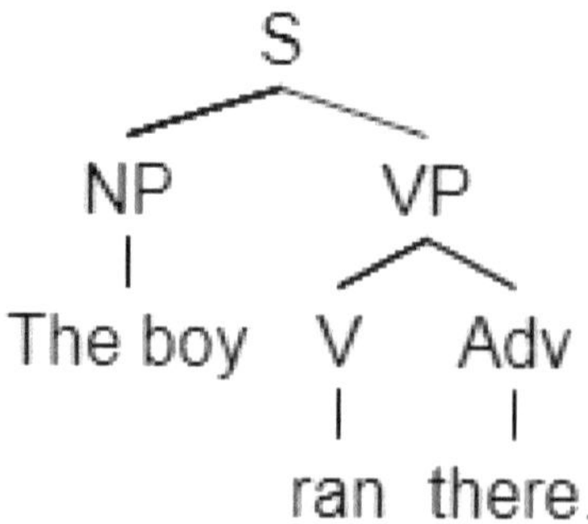

2. Movement:

- Move to the park: To the park, the boy ran. → To the park is a constituent.

Tree Diagram

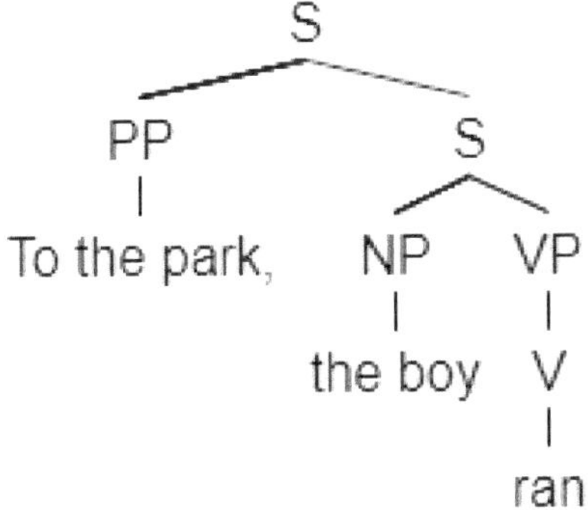

3. Coordination:

- Coordinate The boy: The boy and the girl ran to the park.
- We can coordinate 'the boy' and 'the girl' with the coordinative conjunction 'and'→ so 'the boy' is a constituent.

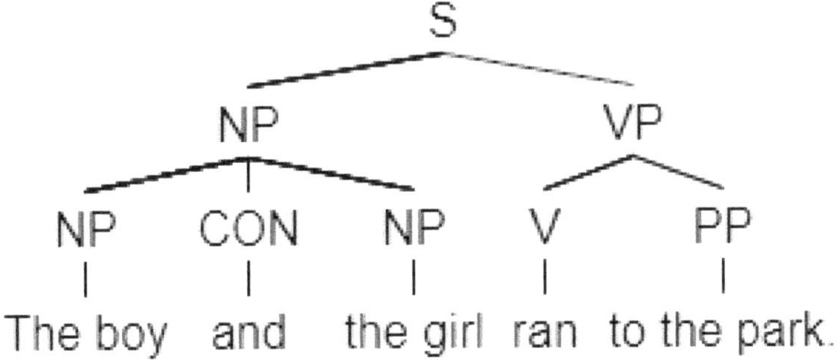

4. Ellipsis:

- Replace 'ran to the park' with 'did': The boy did. → 'Ran to the park' is a constituent.

Tree Diagram:

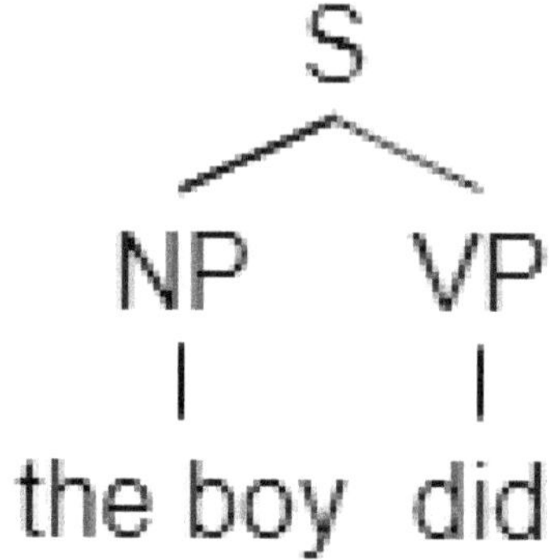

RECURSIVE PROPERTY OF LANGUAGE

The recursive property is one of the most essential features of all languages. It allows repeated usage of the same rules to construct sentences. In addition, it makes the scope of language construction a wider arena and makes it possible to articulate thoughts, emotions and ideas perfectly. We will see how the recursive property of language allows us to embed phrases within phrases and clauses within clauses. In other words, this is the very secret of language, making it capable of constructing and understanding an unlimited number of sentences using limited sources.

In generative grammar, recursion is central to explaining a language's productivity and creativity. It demonstrates how limited resources, such as a finite lexicon and grammar, can generate an endless array of meaningful sentences. This unique feature of language underscores its dynamic and adaptive nature, distinguishing human communication from other forms of symbolic interaction.

Consider language's recursive property as a tool for nesting a multitude of constituents within a sentence using various phrases or clauses.

For example, ...

1. a boy
2. a tall boy
3. a tall black boy
4. a fat, tall black boy
5. a fat, tall young black boy

This way, we can add as many adjectives as possible to describe the "boy". This possibility also grows in infinity, but as our comprehension has a specific limit, we end it somewhere at our convenience.

Observe these examples,

1. a ball
2. a ball in a box
3. a ball in a box on a table
4. a ball in a box on a table in a room
5. a ball in a box on a table in a room in a house...

Here, we have added several prepositional phrases recursively, but the possibilities are open to infinity, which we cannot use.

If we take another example...

1. Tom said it.
2. Ram said that Tom said it.
3. Arjun said that Ram said that Tom said it.
4. Rahim heard Arjun say that Ram said that Tom said it.
5. Babu thought that Rahim heard Arjun say that Ram said that Tom said it.

This way, we can incorporate any clauses as we see fit.

1. Leela bade goodbye to her mother,
2. Leela bade goodbye to her mother, stepped out of the house,
3. Leela bade goodbye to her mother, stepped out of the house, walked towards the gate,
4. Leela bade goodbye to her mother, stepped out of the house, walked towards the gate, pulled open the gate,
5. Leela bade goodbye to her mother, stepped out of the house, walked towards the gate, pulled open the gate, walked straight to the temple...and the nth clause.

We can construct any number of phrases or clauses like this coordinating with the help of coordinating conjunctions.

If the phrase structure is expanded below, almost all the recursions can be rewritten easily.

S→NP+VP

NP→(D)+(AdjP) +(PP) +N

AdjP→ A+NP

VP→V+ (NP) +(AdvP)+(AdjP) +(PP)

AdvP→ Adv+(Adv)+(V)

PP→P +NP

The constituents without brackets are mandatory; in other words, constituents in brackets are optional.

As mentioned earlier, recursion is the process by which linguistic structures (such as phrases or clauses) can embed similar structures within themselves. It allows for the repeated application of a rule, creating layers of complexity within a sentence. For example, a noun phrase (NP) can contain another noun phrase, or a sentence (S) can embed another sentence through complement or relative clauses.

Example:

- Simple sentence: The cat sleeps.
- Recursive addition: The cat that chased the mouse sleeps.
- Further recursion: The cat that chased the mouse that stole the cheese sleeps.

This recursive property allows languages to be infinitely generative despite having a finite vocabulary and a limited set of grammatical rules.

It is fascinating to observe how recursion functions within constituents.

Language consists of hierarchical structures where smaller units (constituents) combine to form larger units. Recursion occurs when:

1. Phrases embed similar phrases:

- Noun Phrases (NPs):
- The book → The book on the table → The book on the table in the library.

- Prepositional Phrases (PPs):
- In the house → In the house with the red roof → In the house with the red roof by the lake.

2. Clauses embedded in other clauses:

- Relative Clauses:
- I know the man→ I know the man who wrote the book→. I know the man who wrote the book that won the prize.
- Complement Clauses:
- He said [that she left]. → He said [that she left because it was late].

3. Coordination:

- Sentences or phrases can recursively join using conjunctions like and or:
- I like apples and oranges.
- I like apples and oranges and bananas.

A closer observation reveals that Recursion is inevitable in Language for many reasons. It enhances the potentiality of expression manifold. As human thoughts and experiences are unlimited, a limited variety of language with a rigid boundary may not reflect them all, but recursions enable him to do so. While human linguistic abilities allow for complex recursive construction, artificial techniques remain more limited in replicating such flexibility. The efficient parsing of recursive structures unburdens cognitive resources from memorising sentence lengths under development. Chiefly, this underscores how recursion streamlines comprehension. Indeed, the capacity for incorporating hierarchical embedding universally underscores language's design for conveying meaning. Such capacity relieves the mind from retaining sequential details while interpreting layered information.

1. Simple to Complex Expansion:

- Base: The boy runs.
- Recursive Addition: The boy who lives next door runs.
- Further: The boy who lives next door and loves pizza runs.

2. Recursive Prepositional Phrases:

- Base: The book is on the table.
- Recursive: The book is on the table by the window in the library.

3. Recursive Clauses:

- Base: She believes [he left].
- Recursive: She believes [he said [she was right]].

Implications of Recursion

1. Infinite Creativity:

Speakers can create and understand sentences they have never encountered before by applying recursive rules.

2. Ambiguity Resolution:

Recursive structures help specify meaning. For example:

Ambiguous Sentence:

"John saw the man with the telescope."

This sentence is ambiguous because it can have two meanings:

1. John is using a telescope to see the man.

2. John saw a man who was holding a telescope.

Using Recursive Structures to Clarify Meaning:

In linguistic terms, recursive structures break sentences into hierarchical components using grammar rules. For example:

Interpretation 1:

S→NP VP

VP→V NP PP

PP→P NP

Breaking it down:

NP: "John"

VP: "Saw [NP [PP [with [the telescope]]]]"

Meaning: "John used the telescope to see."

Interpretation 2:

S→NP VP

VP→V NP

NP→NP PP

PP→P NP

Breaking it down:

NP: "[the man [PP [with [the telescope]]]"

VP: "Saw [NP the man with the telescope]."

Meaning: "John saw a man holding the telescope.

Let us see how recursive Structures Help:

The recursive rules clarify whether "with the telescope" modifies "the man" (Interpretation 2) or "saw" (Interpretation 1). By systematically parsing the sentence into its components, recursive structures remove ambiguity and assign a specific meaning based on the hierarchical relationships.

3. **Cultural and Cognitive Development:**

Recursion lays the groundwork for narratives to blossom, logic to percolate, and contemplations to take flight, each playing a pivotal role in our societal and mental evolution. As evident from our back-and-forth, we inescapably infer that recursion sits at the core of language, owing to how it mirrors language's unbounded creativity. It welcomes limitless reconfigurations of terminology and notions, rendering human intercourse innovative yet malleable in its delivery. Alongside shorter ruminations, complex arrangements of vocabulary weave tales and theories in semantic tapestries whose textures recursively ripple through the corridors of thought, ensuring the endurance of our collective intelligence. The certainty of recursion lies in the hierarchical organisation of language and the universal need for expressive potential. With recursion, language would be expanded and capable of reflecting the complexity of human thought.

We understand that each constituent has enough potential to incorporate as many phrases as possible into the sentence-making process.

Cross-Linguistic Applicability of Phrase Structure Rules

The cross-linguistic applicability of phrase structure rules lies at the heart of generative grammar's goal to uncover universal principles of language. Phrase structure rules provide a systematic framework for analysing the syntax of sentences across languages by breaking them down into hierarchical components, such as noun phrases (NP), verb phrases (VP), and other constituents.

Despite surface-level differences in word order and grammatical structures among languages, such as Subject-Verb-Object (SVO) versus Subject-Object-Verb (SOV) orders, phrase structure rules reveal deep underlying similarities. For example, all languages appear to organise sentences hierarchically rather than linearly, and they conform to principles such as the presence of heads and complements within phrases.

Cross-linguistic studies of syntax have demonstrated that while languages may set different parameters (e.g., head-initial vs. head-final structures), the general framework of phrase structure rules remains applicable. This universality supports the idea of a shared cognitive foundation for language, as posited by Chomsky's Universal Grammar. By adapting phrase structure rules to account for language-specific features, linguists can compare and contrast syntactic patterns, gaining insights into both the universality and diversity of human language.

Until now, we have seen how the components are formed as different phrases and incorporated into the larger ones to become sentences by their recurrent property.

We have seen how language construction is reduced in the generalised phrase structure principles, and they read as follows:

S→NP+VP

NP→(D)+(AdjP) +(PP) +N

AdjP→ Adj+(NP)

VP→V+ (NP) +(AdvP)+(AdjP) +(PP)

AdvP→ Adv+(Adv)+(AdjP)+(V)

PP→P +NP

An infinite number of sentences can be constructed this way, but it does not mean the entirety of the sentences.

The boy saw a snake. (NP+VP=T+N+V+T+N)

The table saw a boy. (NP+VP=T+N+V+T+N)

Both sentences are identical per the phrase structure rules, but the second sentence is nonsensical semantically.

The goats are ready to eat. (NP+VP=T+N+V+PP)

It's a perfect sentence, but it has a very ambiguous meaning. On the one hand, it says that goats are prepared to eat; on the other hand, it says that goats are developed enough to be eaten. The above model does not tell what the speaker meant.

Phrase Structure Grammar (PSG), while helpful in capturing the hierarchical structure of sentences, has several constraints that led to the development of Transformational Generative Grammar (TGG). Here are a few key constraints:

1. **Limited expressiveness**: Phrase structure grammar can struggle with certain syntactic constructs, particularly those involving dependencies such as the relation between subjects and verbs in complex sentences.

2. **Surface structure versus Deep structure:** Phrase structure grammar mainly concerns external constructions that may fail to convey the implicit significances or associations linking components of a sentence entirely. Transformational generative grammar addresses this by distinguishing between underlying implications and surface syntax.

3. **Handling transformations:** Phrase structure regulations inadequately accommodate changes like repositioning - transferring

an object to the start of a sentence, for instance, to emphasise importance - which are pivotal in comprehending sentence variations naturally employed in language.

4. **Ambiguity resolution**: Phrase structure grammar can sometimes produce ambiguous interpretations of a sentence, while TGG provides mechanisms to generate unambiguous structures.

5. **Fixed rules**: The constraints of phrase structure grammar, being overly rigid in the rules, constrain the potential to express the full spectrum of linguistic innovation and diversity seen in natural tongues. While the precepts highlighted a requirement for a more pliable and inclusive structure, Transformational Grammar and Generative Semantics aim to furnish this by encapsulating transformational directives and underlying frameworks.

Synopsis of the chapter

In essence, phrase structure grammar provides a foundational framework for understanding how sentences in a language are built. By recognising that language exhibits a hierarchical structure where smaller units (words) combine to form larger units (phrases) and, ultimately, sentences, we can begin to formalise our understanding of the recurring patterns and constraints that govern linguistic expression. The identification of constituents through various tests allows us to delve deeper into the internal organisation of sentences, revealing the underlying relationships between words and their groupings. This framework, with its focus on phrases such as noun phrases, verb phrases, and others, provides a crucial stepping stone towards a more comprehensive understanding of the intricate mechanisms that drive human language.

The key concepts covered in the chapter on phrase structure grammar are:

1. Phrase Structure: The hierarchical organisation of sentences, where smaller units combine to form larger ones.
2. Recurring Property of Language: The observation that language exhibits consistent patterns in how words are grouped.
3. Constituents: Groups of words that function as a single unit within a sentence.
4. Different Phrases: The various types of phrases that can be identified within a sentence, such as noun phrases, verb phrases, prepositional phrases, etc.
5. Constituent Tests: Methods used to identify the constituent structure of a sentence.
6. Cross-Linguistic Applicability: phrase structure provides ample information to assess the universality of linguistic structures.
7. Constraints of Phrase Structure: The limitations and rules that govern how phrases can be formed and combined within a sentence.

This chapter effectively encapsulates the core ideas of phrase structure grammar and its significance in understanding the structure and organisation of human language.

CHAPTER II

TRANSFORMATIONAL GENERATIVE GRAMMAR

"The inability of surface structure to indicate semantically significant grammatical relations (i.e., serve as deep structure) is one fundamental fact that motivated the development of transformational generative grammar, in both its classical and modern varieties" (Topics in the theory of generative grammar, Noam Chomsky page 17)

At the end of the first chapter, we saw some of the significant constraints of Phrase Structure Grammar (PSG), which paved the way for Transformational Generative Grammar (TGG). Now, the task ahead is to perceive the same thing, and for seamless comprehension, we should know some new concepts that we have not discussed so far.

In his structural linguistics, Ferdinand de Saussure, one of the great names in linguistics, put forward two concepts, namely 'langue' and 'parole'. According to him, langue is the structure, and all language principles and parole is the language that the speaker has pronounced. These are more or less the concepts used as new terminology, "competence" and "performance", of which Noam Chomsky speaks and from which he develops- language and E-language.

To better comprehend structured, pronounced, and apprehended language, Noam Chomsky divides its structure into two levels: the surface structure and the deep structure.

SURFACE STRUCTURE AND DEEP STRUCTURE

Beforehand, I say this: just like in the case of the word "generative" in generative grammar, we should not take the words "deep" and "surface" literally. In generative grammar, 'generative' shows the ability of descriptiveness rather than generativity or generativeness, though there is an element that generates it. Similarly, if we consider that something in-depth and something on the surface is superficial, we are somewhat away from concepts.

To get to the point, the language in the abstract form is the deep structure, a theoretical representation of the underlying meaning of a sentence, and the concrete is the surface structure. In other words, when I say, "I can swim", this pronounced part is the surface structure, where all the unexpressed parts, which are all the possible sentences of the same subject, are deep structures.

What distinguishes transformational generative grammar from phrase structure grammar is its ability to transform sentences and restrict errors in generating legitimate sentences from natural language.

Let us delve into this in detail now. When we discussed phrase structure, we saw how infinite sentences are generated within the framework of finite components. This is the model of the mechanism, albeit with limitations, that the human brain uses to construct and understand natural language. To overcome these limitations and further expand the reach of finding grammars that fit the set of entire sentences in a given language, Chomsky proposes Transformational Generative Grammar. This is a significant advancement, as it allows us to transform sentences and restrict errors in generating legitimate sentences from natural language. There are three key components: syntactic components, semantic components, and phonological components. Semantic components directly imply semantic structures in the deep structure, while phonological components interpret the syntactic structure in the surface structure. Now, we need to examine in detail how these components work and overcome the ineffectiveness of the phrase structure. Firstly, language is a tool to express concepts, feelings, emotions, and thoughts from one person to others as explicitly as possible. All these are exclusively related to the mind until they are expressed through expressions after various processing activities. Other factors that influence expressions, while minimal, are external stability and instantaneous organising capacity. A person, no matter how competent, may not use their language skills or may not even be able to use them. Thus, language competence has practically no value in the construction or grammar of the language. Here is the significance of Transformational Generative Grammar.

When I say, "I can swim", the pronounced part is the surface structure, but prior to being the surface structure, the core component undergoes several changes or transformations. "I" and "swim" together. "I swim" is the essential component, and its performed form is "I can swim". One can assume here that there are many things left and that there are some additions. For instance, how can I swim? Very well or just. Where do I swim? In a pool, river or sea? Who am I here? An adult or a child? How do I learn to swim? Self or trained? When will I swim? Is it morning or night? Am I a hobbyist or a professional? As mentioned above, many uncompressed parts are associated with the base components. Despite all these options, the speaker or his psychic core, half consciously and half instinctively, transformed the basic idea as "I can swim". This process of transformation, which is deeply rooted in the human mind, showcases the immense power of human cognition in language construction and comprehension.

If I elaborate further, consider this analogy: I may know the fundamental principles of multiplication, but that does not automatically mean I can multiply several numbers at once. I need a piece of paper and a pencil to calculate and follow several procedures to transform the raw numbers into the product. In this example, my knowledge is my competence, which does not provide the answer, but the procedures do, meaning the transformation results in the surface structure. Similarly, in the case of language, competence and transformational procedures are the inherent parts of a man's psychic order that create and include novel and infinite sentences. These transformational procedures, when applied systematically, bring order and logic to the process of language transformation, highlighting the systematic nature of transformation rules.

KERNEL SENTENCES

A sentence before any transformations take place is said to be a kernel or matrix sentence. This is a simple, affirmative, declarative, and active sentence that represents the core component. It serves as a starting point for understanding more complex sentence structures. Apart from these, all other types of sentences are transformed in one manner or another.

For instance, the sentence 'The girl opened the door' is a core sentence, meeting all the conditions, and the idea cannot be further divided. However, if we say, 'The door is green', the concept can be split into 'there is a door' and 'it is green', making it a non-kernel sentence.

The girl did not open the gate. (Negative; non-kernel)

Did the girl open the door? (Question; non-kernel)

It was the girl who opened the door. (Clause; non-kernel)

The girl opened the door, but her brother closed it. (Compound; non-kernel)

The girl opened the door to move out. (PRO; non-kernel)

The girl opened the door, not her brother. (Deletion; non-kernel)

The door was opened by the girl (Passive, non-kernel)

T-RULES

Now, we will see how transformation rules work with English sentences.

In Transformational Generative Grammar (TGG), transformations are rules (T-Rules) that operate on a sentence's underlying deep structure to derive its surface structure. These transformations alter the arrangement of words and phrases while preserving the sentence's core meaning.

We have seen that Deep Structure is the abstract, underlying representation of a sentence that encodes its grammatical relationships and consists of essential components.

- Example: "The boy eats the apple"

The Surface Structure is the actual spoken or written form of the sentence after any transformational rules are applied.

- Example: "Does the boy eat the apple?" After applying the T-Rules of the question, here is what the Surface Structure looks like.

Let us examine the different types of transformational rules.

1. **Affix hopping** is a technique that involves attaching inflectional properties to the main verb to meet agreement features and to create past tense, negative, or questions.

- Examples:
- Deep structure: "He + past + eat"
- Surface structure: "He ate"
- Deep structure: "They + past + be + working.
- Surface structure: "They were working"

2. **Do-support** is another process that inserts 'do' in a sentence where tense, agreement, or negation cannot be directly attached to the verb.

- Example:
- Deep structure: "He not eats."
- Surface structure: "He does not eat."

3. **Wh-Movement** is the next T-rule, where the Wh-word moves to the front of a sentence to form a question.

- Example:
- Deep structure: "You are reading what"
- Surface structure: "What are you reading?"

4. **Passivisation** is a transformation rule where the object of the verb takes the subject position of the sentence, and the verb turns into the 'be + past participle' form.

- Example:
- Deep structure: "The dog chased the cat"
- Surface structure: "The cat was chased by the dog"

Some more examples with Tree Diagrams

Example 1: Affix Hopping

Deep Structure: S → NP + T + VP

- Subject: "He"
- Tense: "past"
- Verb: "eat"
- Transformation: Attach "past" to "eat".
- Surface Structure: "He ate."

Tree Diagram:

S
NP VP
He V
ate

Example 2: Wh-Movement

- Deep Structure: "You will eat what"

Tree Diagram (Deep Structure)

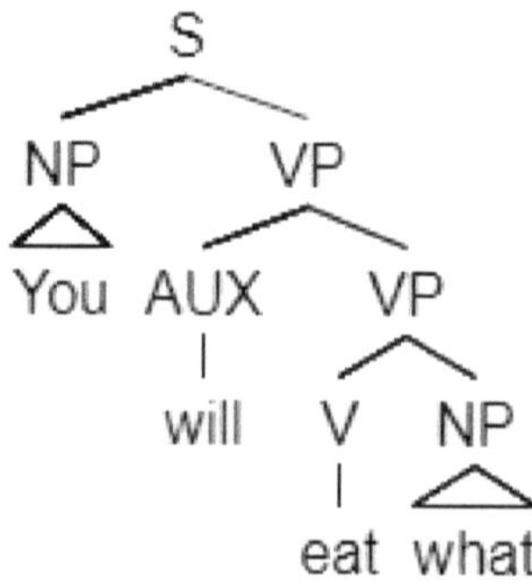

- Transformation: Move "what" to the beginning of the sentence.
- Surface Structure: "What will you eat?"

Tree Diagram (Surface Structure):

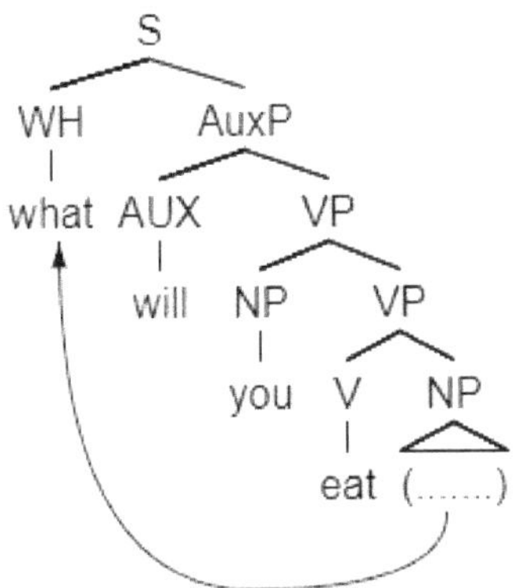

1. Passive Transformation

- Function: The object of the verb takes the subject position of the sentence, and the verb turns into the 'be + past participle' form.
- Example:
- Active: (Deep structure) The cat chased the mouse.
- Passive: (Surface structure) The mouse was chased by the cat.

Tree diagram active:

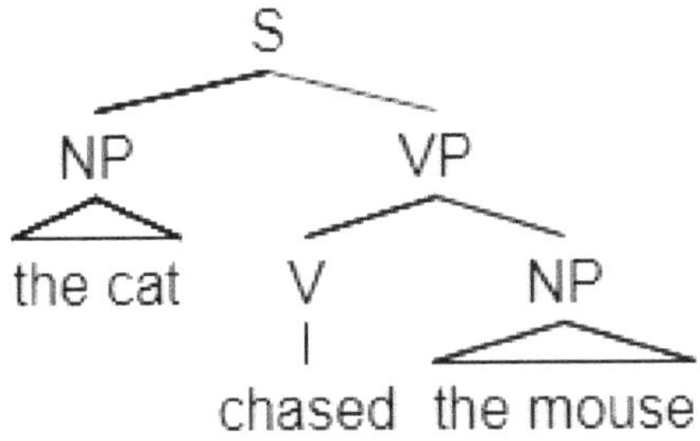

Tree diagram passive

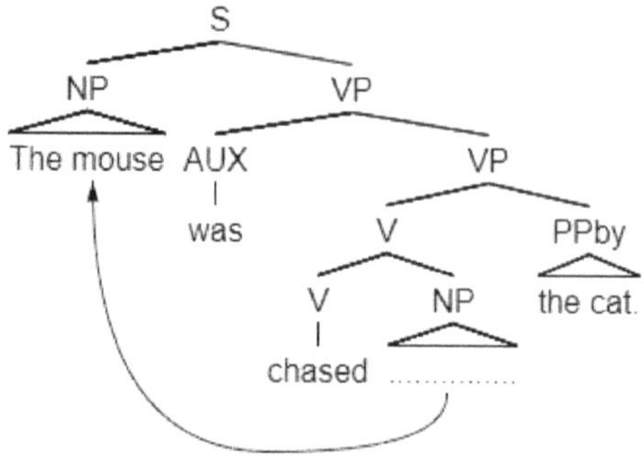

2. Question Transformation (Yes/No Questions)

- Function: The auxiliary moves to the front of the sentence to form a question.
- Example:
- Declarative: The boy is playing chess.

Tree Diagram before movement takes place.

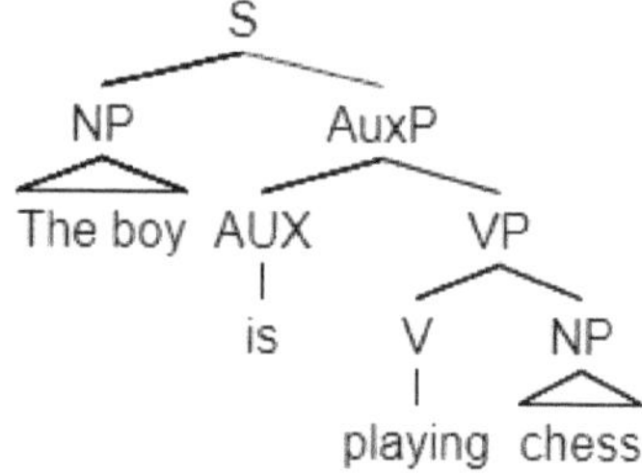

Tree Diagram after movement.

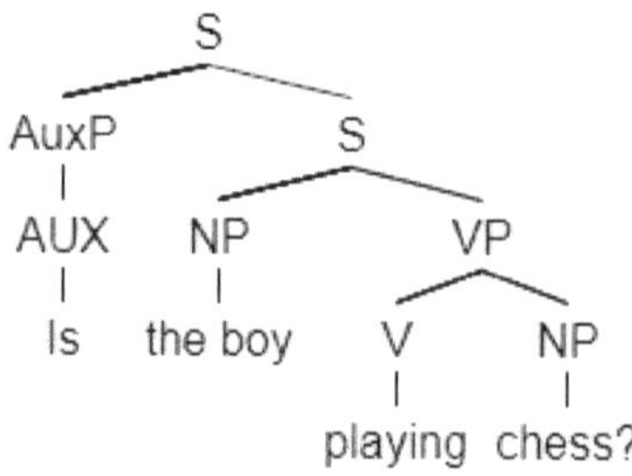

3. Wh-Question Transformation

- Function: Transforms a declarative sentence into a wh-question (e.g., who, what, where, when, why, how).
- Example:
- Declarative: The boy is playing in the park.

Tree Diagram before the transformation:

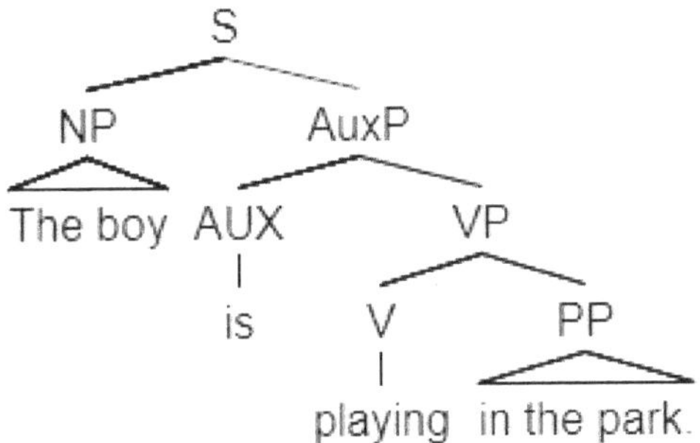

Tree Diagram after the transformation:

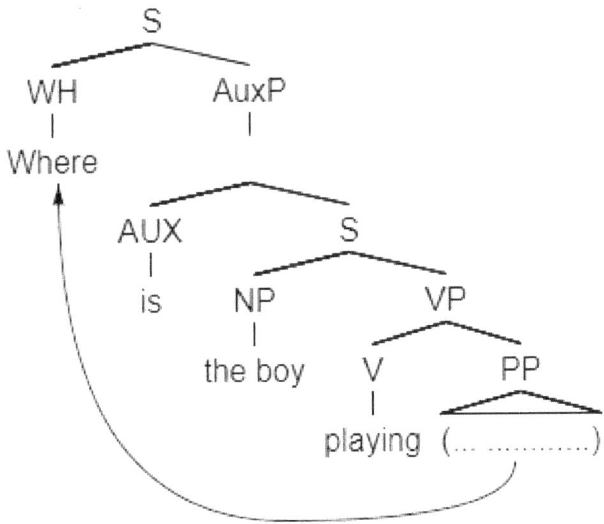

Where is the boy playing?

4. Negation Transformation

Do-Support:

- Function: Introduces negation into a sentence after applying 'Do support' when tense or agreement cannot be directly attached to the verb.
- Example:
- Affirmative: The girl likes ice cream.
- Negative: The girl does not like ice cream.

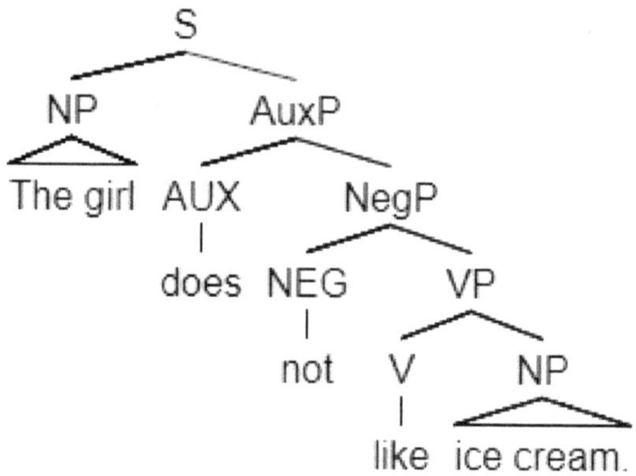

5. Embedding Transformation

- Function: Integrates one sentence into another as a subordinate clause.
- Example:
- Simple Sentence: The boy said something.
- Embedded Sentence: The boy said that he was going to the store.

Tree diagram

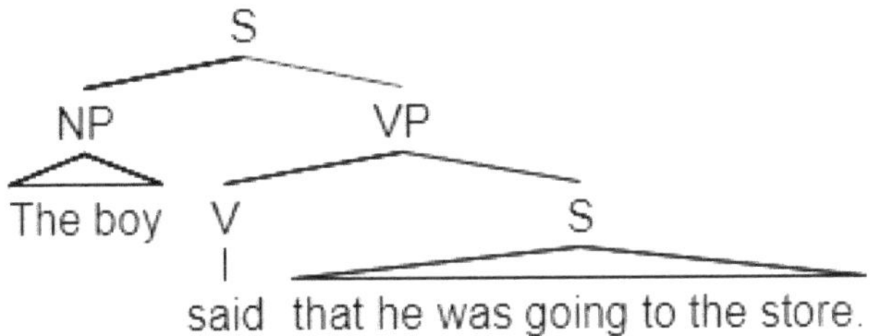

Significance of Transformations

Transformations play a crucial role in understanding how a sentence's deep structure is mapped onto its surface structure. They explain the relationship between different sentence types, such as active and passive, declarative and interrogative, and affirmative and negative. It is quite interesting that different kinds of sentences share the same deep structure, but they appear to have different surface structures after applying the T-rules.

While the examples that we discussed earlier illustrate some common types of transformations, it is important to remember that the specific set of transformations may vary depending on the language and theoretical framework used.

From the discussions in this chapter, we understand that Transformational Generative Grammar has secured a prime place in the history of GG following its inception and subsequent developments. However, TGG could not address many of the issues related to the construction and apprehension of language. Evidence piled up and raised many questions regarding the competency of TGG's theories. Now, our focus will be on the important constraints and limitations of TGG and how they led to the evolution of Generative Grammar and the introduction of X-Bar theory.

Although influential, the theories of Deep structure and transformations were criticised for their abstract nature and lack of practical evidence in literature and psychology. Furthermore, they witnessed the generation of numerous ungrammatical sentences unless restrictions were placed on them. The next issue was their utter negligence of semantical and structural relationships. Many linguists suggested Generative Semantics, a set of new theories, as an alternative to address the issues regarding the limitations of TGG that failed to address semantic problems. As universal properties of language became less significant in TGG, the cross-linguistic applicability of transformation rules became uncertain.

Generative grammar has consistently argued for the importance of language acquisition and syntax in aiding human children in achieving success. However, many theories related to TGG failed to gather evidence that they really helped children.

To put it in brief, transformational generative grammar's limitations and constraints were its overgeneration of sentences, lack of empirical evidence, and universal applicability. These constraints highlighted the need for a more consistent and universal representation of syntactic structures across different languages. In the coming chapters, we will see how generative grammar overcame these limitations by introducing new frameworks and theories, such as the X-Bar theory and the Government and Binding theory.

To substantiate the points that we discussed, we are now looking into a few examples.

1. Lack of Uniformity in Phrase Structure

- In TGG, phrase structure rules (PSRs) were language-specific and could vary significantly between languages.
- For example:

Here is an example of how PSRs differ between English and Hindi, two languages with different word order conventions:

1. Example in English (SVO - Subject-Verb-Object Language)

"The boy eats an apple."

Phrase Structure Rule:

Derivation:

- [NP [Det "The"] [N "boy"]] [VP [V "eats"] [NP [Det "an"] [N "apple"]]]

Tree diagram:

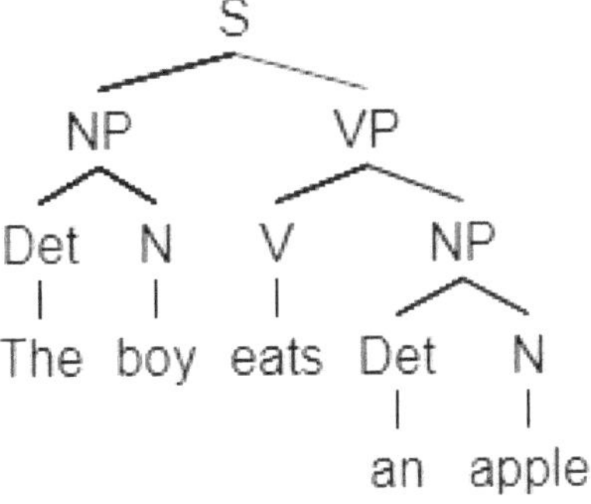

- The Subject (S) precedes the Verb (V), and the Object (O) follows the verb, following the SVO order.

2. Example in Hindi (SOV - Subject-Object-Verb Language)

लड़का सेब खाता है।

(Laṛkā seb khātā hai.)

"The boy eats an apple."

Phrase Structure Rule:

Derivation:

- [S [NP [N "⍰⍰⍰⍰⍰" (Laṛkā)] [Det –]] [VP [NP [N "⍰⍰⍰" (Seb)]] [V "⍰⍰⍰⍰ ⍰⍰" (Khātā hai)]]

Tree diagram:

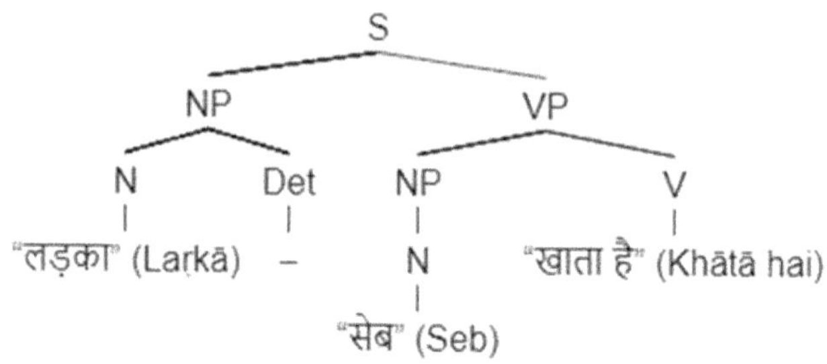

- In Hindi, the Subject (S) comes first, the Object (O) comes next, and the Verb (V) appears at the end, following the SOV order.

Key Difference

- English (SVO): The Verb precedes the object within the VP.
- Hindi (SOV): The Verb comes after the object within the VP.

This language-specific variation in phrase structure rules demonstrates why a universal grammar must allow for such differences while maintaining an overarching framework for comparison.

- This lack of a uniform representation made it challenging to describe the universal properties of language.
- The X-bar theory addresses this by introducing a universal template for phrase structure that applies across languages.

TGG's overdependence on transformations

- Transformational grammar formulated by TGG was overly dependent on rules to generate surface structures from underlying representations, sometimes leading to complicated derivations.
- Certain linguistic phenomena, such as movement or adjunction, demanded multiple successive transformations under TGG.
- The advent of X-bar theory reduces dependence on transformations by offering a more hierarchical and modular architecture in which phrases are built step-by-step from their constituents.

3. Difficulty in Capturing Intermediate Structures

- Traditional TGG lacked an intermediate level of syntactic representation between lexical items and fully expanded phrases.
- For example, it could not distinguish between:
- Head (e.g., "read")
- Phrase (e.g., "read a book")
- The solution was to introduce intermediate projections in X-bar theory, which bridged the gap between individual words (heads) and whole phrases.

4. Need for Cross-Linguistic Generalization

- TGG was unable to give a satisfactory explanation for the universality of certain syntactic patterns, such as the hierarchical structure of phrases or the relationship between heads and their complements.

We will see in the forthcoming chapters how the X_bar schema addresses it

- The X-bar theory provides a universal schema:
- All phrases are built around a head
- Phrases follow a consistent structure:
- Intermediate projection.
- Maximal projection.
- Specifier and complement positions.

5. Ambiguity in Binary Branching

- TGG did not strictly require splitting nodes into binary branching, permitting various structures to form without guidelines.
- For example:
- Certain arrangements were flat, whereas others were binary with intermediate nodes, and this frequently caused confusion and intricacy.
- X-bar theory necessitates splitting each node precisely into binary, ensuring uniformly arranged hierarchies.

6. Limited Explanation for Head-Complement Relations

- Traditional Generative Grammar lacked a structured way to fully explain the linguistic relations between a headword and the other parts joined to it.
- X-bar theory logically defines these relations:
- The head projects its characteristics to the phrase.
- Complements are intimately connected to the head, while the adjuncts of the phrase sit in a higher place within the overarching syntactic frame.

- We will also see that in further evolution, the theory of government and binding will provide more clarity on the relationship issue.

7. Inadequate Representation of Recursion

- While TGG recognised recursion as a defining characteristic of language, it lacked a cohesive framework for depicting this quality through phrase structure rules.
- The X-bar theory permits recursive projections.
- A complement can itself be a complex syntactic unit containing further embedded phrases or subordinate clauses.

Conclusion

While the TGG addressed syntactic relationships, it failed to capture the rich hierarchical structure of language and account for cross-linguistic generalisations. The X-bar theory rectified these deficiencies by positing a uniform phrase structure schema with intermediate and maximum projections. The X-Bar schema has made it possible to define constituent types productively based on their position relative to heads, and universal structures can have consistent projections of the head and other constituents. By removing language-particular machinery in favour of a strictly configurational architecture, the X-bar framework elevated linguistic theory to a higher level of theoretical elegance and empirical adequacy. It established the foundation for much of contemporary work in syntax by demonstrating the explanatory value of abstract, modular representations based on universal constraints on syntactic form.

Synopsis of the chapter

Transformational Generative Grammar (TGG) is a theory of syntax that explains the deep and surface structures of sentences and the transformations that connect them. It succeeded in solving the deficiencies of Phrase Structure Grammar (PSG) and provides a formal system to describe how human languages generate grammatically correct sentences from abstract representations.

1. Deep Structure and Surface Structure

- Deep Structure: Represents the abstract, underlying syntactic organisation of a sentence. It encodes the core grammatical relationships, such as subject-verb-object.
- Surface Structure: The Actual spoken or written form of a sentence after transformations have been applied to the deep structure.
- Example: Deep structure "The boy eats the apple" transforms into the surface structure "Does the boy eat the apple?" for a question.

2. Transformational Rules (T-Rules)

a. Do-Support

- Inserts "do" to form negatives, questions, or emphatic statements when there is no auxiliary verb.
- Example:
- Deep Structure: "He not eats"
- Surface Structure: "He does not eat."

b. Auxiliary Fronting for Questions

- Moves auxiliary verbs to the beginning of a sentence to form questions.
- Example:

- Deep Structure: "You are reading a book."
- Surface Structure: "Are you reading a book?"

c. Negative Formation

- Adds "not" after an auxiliary verb or introduces "do-support" if no auxiliary is present.
- Example:
- Deep Structure: "He sings."
- Surface Structure: "He does not sing."

d. Wh-Movement for Questions

- Moves a "wh"-word (e.g., who, what, where) to the front of a sentence for question formation.
- Example:
- Deep Structure: "You are reading what"
- Surface Structure: "What are you reading?"

e. Transformation of Past Tenses

- Applies tense markers to verbs during transformations, often involving affixation or modification.
- Example:
- Deep Structure: "He + past + walk"
- Surface Structure: "He walked."

f. Passivation

- Moves the object of an active sentence to the subject position and adjusts the verb phrase.
- Example:

- Deep Structure: "The dog chased the cat"
- Surface Structure: "The cat was chased by the dog."

g. Embedding a Sentence in a Sentence

- Allows subordinate clauses to be embedded within main clauses.
- Example:
- "The boy knows" + "The girl is singing"
- Surface Structure: "The boy knows that the girl is singing."

h. Deletion

- Removes redundant or implied elements in sentences.
- Example:
- Deep Structure: "She said she would come."
- Surface Structure: "She said she will"

3. Importance of Transformational Rules

T-Rules are essential for bridging the gap between the Universal Grammar (UG) shared across languages (deep structure) and the specific grammar of individual languages (surface structure). They account for variations in sentence types, such as questions, negations, and passives, while maintaining grammaticality.

Conclusion

TGG provides a systematic framework for understanding how humans generate and comprehend language. Transformational rules like do-support, auxiliary fronting, wh-movement, and passivation illustrate how simple, universal grammatical structures are transformed into complex surface-level sentences across languages. Although Transformational Generative grammar (TGG) is a beneficial theory for Generative grammar, it over-generates sentences due to several constraints. This led to the inclusion of the X-Bar theory, which will be discussed in the next chapter.

CHAPTER III

X-BAR SCHEMA

So far, we have discussed phrase structure grammar (PSG) and Transformational Generative Grammar (TGG) in our previous chapters with a minimum target to understand the mental grammar structure. In saying minimum target, we attempt to understand the mechanism that helps a child learn their language at least in the minimum. According to the grammar we discussed earlier, sentences are not merely a string of words. Words are formed in phrases to formulate larger components to make sentences. Phrase structure helps us with the basic structure of a sentence, and transformational generative grammar describes how kernel sentences are transformed by expanding the range of well-formed sentences. Thus, a grammatical theory explains the mechanism of the mind that helps shape the correct sentences in each language. The flaw of a grammatical theory is the possibility of forming ill-formed sentences. And, of course, the grammar of a language lies in the intuitive mechanism of a native user to comprehend and create legitimate sentences.

In simple terms, the X-Bar theory is the generalised abstraction of the common structural forms of a language's mental grammar. It not only simplifies sentence structure but also addresses issues related to the semantic relationships of phrases that have not been resolved in PSG and TGG.

Modern linguists rely more on morphological, phonological, and distributional evidence than vague definitions to categorise words. The lexical categories such as nouns, verbs, prepositions, adverbs and adjectives, functional categories like Determiners, and inflectional categories like modals are important word categories. Noun Phrases, Verb Phrases, and Prepositional phrases are phrasal categories. This approach helps to analyse the structural hierarchical relationships of words and phrases that constitute a sentence.

We have already seen that the properties of phrases are like the head of the phrases. This means that a verb phrase must contain at least one verb, which is the head of the phrase, and it exerts the categorical properties of the head. The properties of each category are also helpful for language acquisition in many ways. For example, when we say that nouns have plurals, it is the property of the category, and what remains is to set the rules to make the plurals.

Let us now consider how X-Bar theory overcomes many of the constraints of PSG and TGG and simplifies generative grammar. The structure of a sentence that we have seen so far is

S➔NP VP

The boy hit the ball.

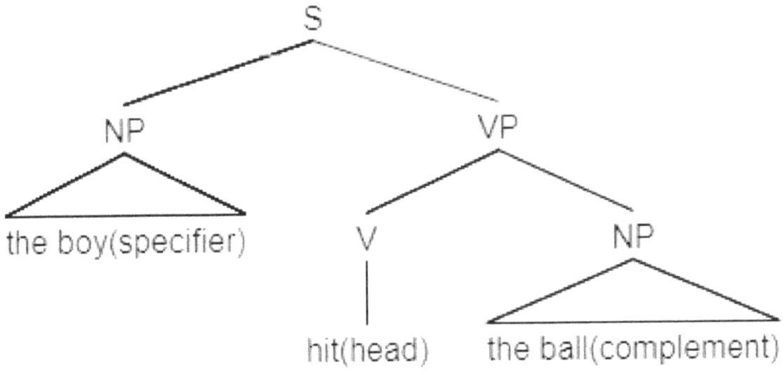

The NP "the boy" acts as a VP specifier in which the headword is hit, and the NP "the ball" acts as the complement to the same.

Now let us consider an NP "the boy from the village".

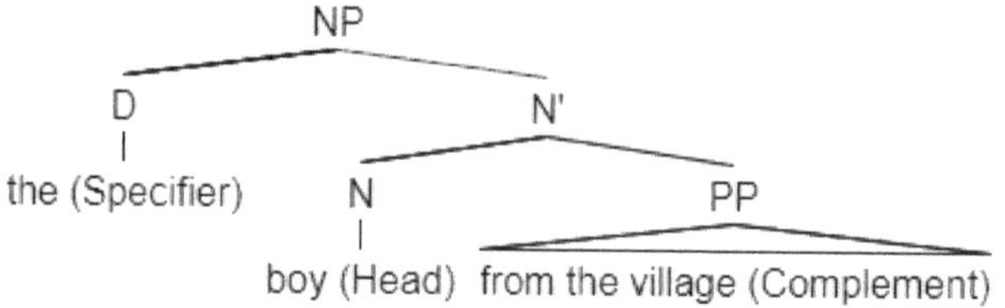

In this case, the determiner 'the' becomes the specifier of the headword 'boy', which falls left, and the PP 'from the village' complements the same. The intermediate node N'(pronounced as N-bar) is a sister node to the specifier and a daughter node to the NP. Similarly, the headword 'boy' is the daughter node of N' and the sister node of PP.

Now consider the VP 'seldom drink wine.'

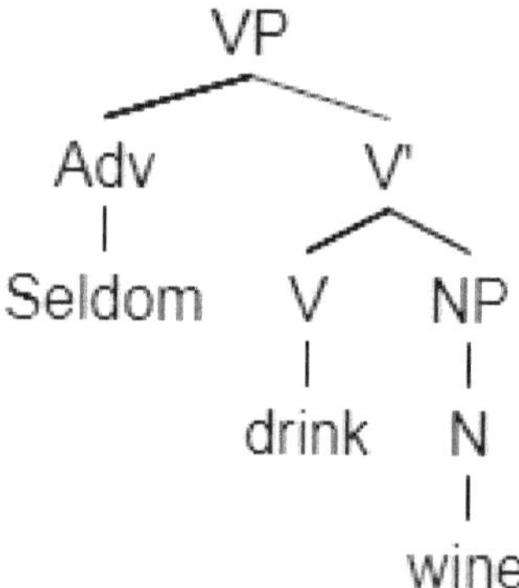

The VP also has a structure identical to that of the NP and S. Drink (V) is the head of the phrase, while the adverb seldom acts as a specifier, and the noun wine becomes the complement of the head.

Even if the VP consists of a clause, the structure would be identical, but a clause acts as a complement.

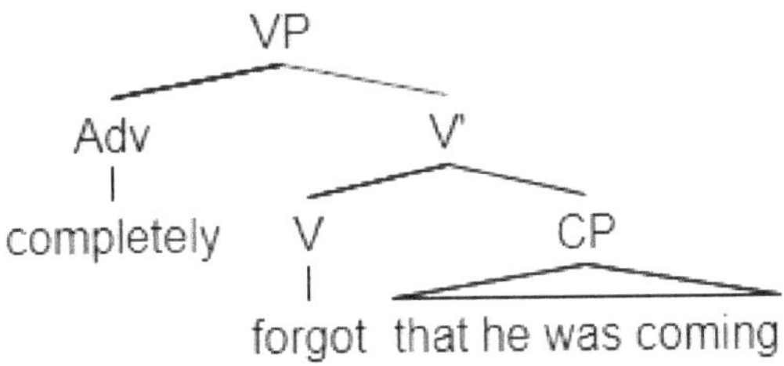

In the example, the verb forgot is the head having an adverb that completely acts as a specifier, and the clause 'that he was coming' is a complement.

Now, consider an AdjP (Adjective Phrase) 'very tall and strong.'

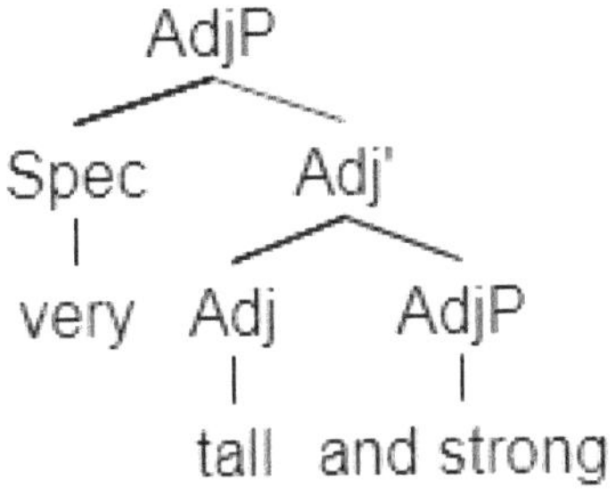

Let us see a Prepositional Phrase: "In the beautiful park."

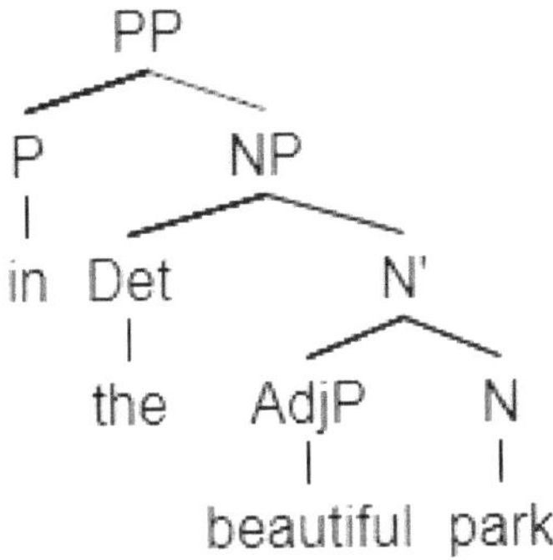

Now let's see what an Adverb Phrase (AdvP) look like:

'quite quickly'

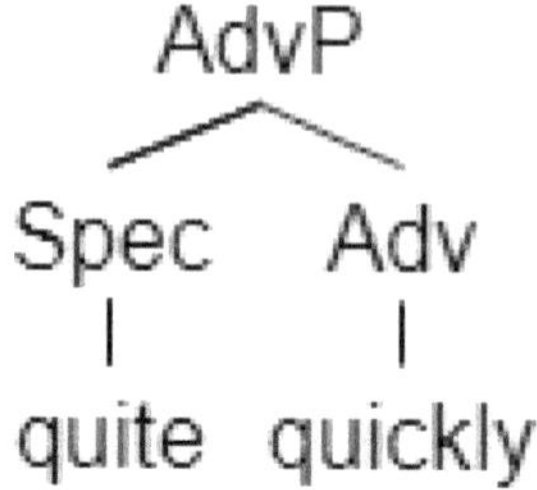

A close examination reveals that all phrasal categories, including sentences, are similarly structured. If we sum up the abstraction of similarity, it will be as follows:

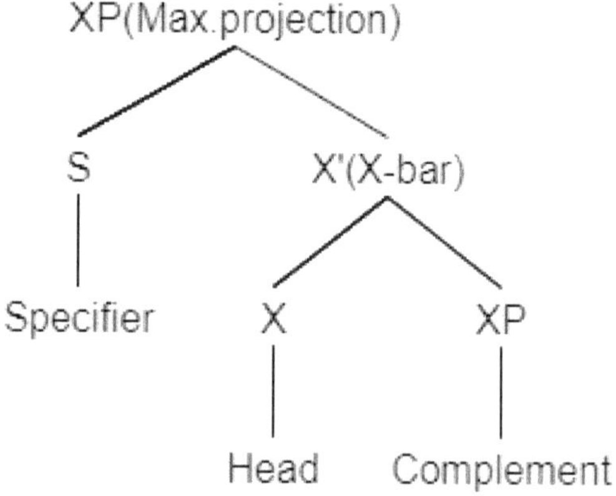

The X-bar template is used to represent the hierarchical structure of phrases in syntax. It captures the universal organisation of phrases across languages. At the core of this structure is the maximum projection (XP), which is the largest unit of the phrase, such as a Noun Phrase (NP), Verb Phrase (VP), or Adjective Phrase (AdjP). The XP dominates all other elements in the phrase and serves as its full representation. Inside the XP, the specifier is a position that often modifies or narrows the interpretation of the phrase. Below the specifier is the intermediate projection (X'), pronounced "X-bar," which mediates between the head of the phrase and its complement. The head (X) is the core (Head) of the phrase, such as a verb in a VP, a noun in an NP, or an adjective in an AdjP, and determines the phrase's category. The complement is a phrase that completes the meaning of the head. The X-bar structure is recursive and allows for embedding and modification, creating a consistent framework for understanding phrase structure in natural languages.

In the case of the inclusion of an adjunct (indirect object in traditional grammar), the number of intermediate bar levels will be increased to accommodate it. This is the way it will be.

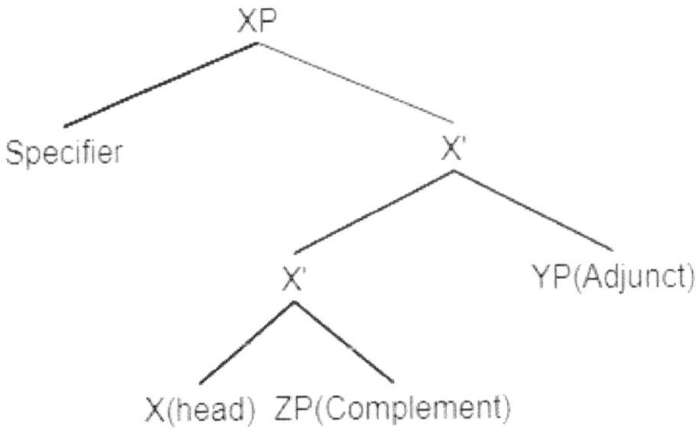

In a broad meaning, specifiers, adjuncts, and complements are modifiers in one way or another, but their positions are quite different. A specifier is the daughter of an XP and sister to an X', an adjunct is a daughter of an X' and sister to an X', and a complement is a daughter of an X' and sister to an X (the head)

When considering a sentence, the maximum projection is seen in IP (Inflectional Phrase). This shows the relation between the phrases (constituents) and the independent nature of the inflexion in the sentence. This will be discussed further at a future opportunity.

STRUCTURAL RELATIONS

At this juncture, it is better to understand the technicality of specific terms such as branching, domination, immediate domination, etc. Branching is the dividing up of a node into more. 'Domination means a node is in a hierarchically higher position than others. The 'A' dominates other nodes in the pictorial example. Immediate domination refers to a particular node, and no other intermediate node exists between them.

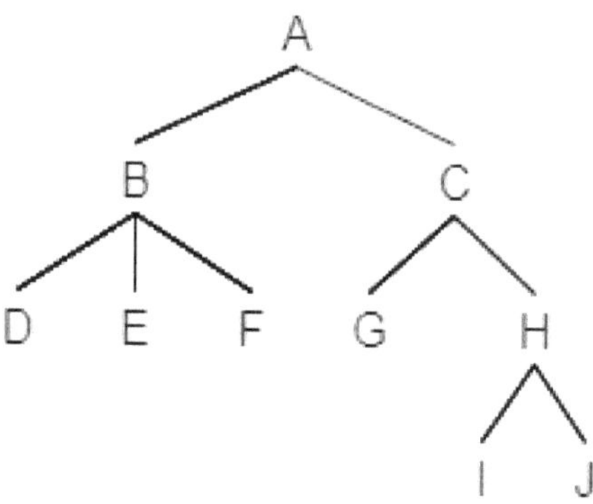

We have seen earlier and that in the above diagram, A refers to the maximal projection. Simultaneously, A is the mother node at B and C, and B and C are sister nodes. D, E, F, G, I, &J are terminal nodes since there are no longer any branches for them. B, C, &H are intermediate nodes because they have a middle position between the upper and lower nodes.

When we say that X dominates Y, it means that if and only if X is in a higher position, it dominates each node until Y.

As per this definition, we can rewrite the above diagram as

A dominates B, C, D, E, F, G, H, I, & J

B dominates D, E, &F

C dominates G, H, I, &J

H dominates I, &J

In any case, the dominant node and the nodes dominated together make a field, a component of the sentence. And it is equally clear that outside of these areas, not two or more elements make a constituent.

If we apply generative rules, we will see.

A→B C

B→D E F

C→G H

H→I J

Since D, E, F, G, I, &J are the terminal nodes, they also represent the word labels of all categories, including lexical, functional, and inflectional. So, we can rewrite the tree above as "the young boy hit the ball".

The above discussion clearly shows that In X-bar theory, syntactic categories are crucial for understanding how different components of sentences are structured and interact. Each category can be broken down using the X-bar schema, which helps describe the internal organisation of phrases. One needs a thorough understanding of the major syntactic categories to move further, so let us summarise it with a few more examples:

1. Noun Phrases (NP)

Nouns are the heads of noun phrases. They can include specifiers like determiners or possessive pronouns and complements like prepositional phrases or adjective phrases.

- Example: In the phrase "the quick brown fox," "fox" is the head noun (N), "the" is a specifier, and "quick brown" are adjectives serving as adjuncts. The structure is:

NP -> D' (D = the) + N' (N' -> AdjP (quick, brown) + N (fox))

2. Verb Phrases (VP)

Verbs are the heads of verb phrases. These phrases can contain specifiers (less common in English), complements such as direct objects or prepositional phrases, and adjuncts like adverbs.

- Example: In "John was reading a book quietly," "was reading" is the head verb (V), "a book" is a complement (NP), and "quietly" is an adjunct (AdvP). The structure is:

VP -> V' (V' -> V (was reading) + NP (a book)) + AdvP (quietly)

3. Adjective Phrases (AdjP)

Adjectives function as heads of adjective phrases. These can be modified by adverbs or lead to complement prepositional phrases.

- Example: In "incredibly happy with the result," "happy" is the adjective head, "incredibly" is an adverb modifying the adjective, and "with the result" is a compliment. The structure is:

AdjP -> AdvP (incredibly) + Adj' (Adj' -> Adj (happy) + PP (with the result))

4. Prepositional Phrases (PP)

Prepositions head prepositional phrases. These phrases typically include the preposition and its object, which is usually a noun phrase.

- Example: In "on the table," "on" is the head preposition (P), and "the table" is the complement (NP). The structure is:

PP -> P' (P' -> P (on) + NP (the table))

5. Adverb Phrases (AdvP)

Adverbs are heads of adverb phrases. These can be standalone or modified by other adverbs.

- Example: In "very quickly," "quickly" is the head adverb (Adv), and "very" is a modifying adverb. The structure is:

AdvP -> Adv' (Adv' -> Adv (very) + Adv (quickly))

Minor Categories:

These include Determiner Phrases (DP) and Quantifier Phrases (QP), which serve specific syntactic functions:

Determiners (like "the" and "a") often head DPs, especially in languages where they play a prominent role in phrase structure. (The Determiner phrase—DP needs more clarification, and we will discuss this next under a specific subheading, namely DP Hypothesis.)

Quantifiers (like "all" and "every") head QPs and specify a quantity.

Examples for Minor Categories:

DP: "The large dog" could be analysed where "the" is a determiner heading a DP that includes an NP ("large dog").

QP: In "all these books," "all" is a quantifier modifying "these books," structuring it as QP -> Q' (Q' -> Q (all) + DP (these books)).

It is worthwhile to note that each phrase follows the same structural patterns, reflecting the head as the core and specifier, complement and adjunct to modify it. All the components are arranged hierarchically, revealing their relationships explicitly. This helps to analyse the structural relationships and properties of the phrase.

DP HYPOTHESIS

X-bar theory, in a particular way, encourages and, to some extent, consolidates the notion that the NP is a DP (Determiner Phrase). As per this, the Determiner is the head rather than the Noun.

Let us look at the arguments before coming to an early conclusion.

To begin with, all heads fall to the left when the tree diagram is made for a phrase, except in the case of a Noun Phrase. However, it is too weak an argument to be counted since no such rule exists. However, the distributional position causes doubt about whether the Determiner occupies a specifier position or the Noun occupies the complement position.

From the discussion, we understand that anything that is not a head must be a phrase. It creates an issue for an NP when we say a noun is the head. For instance, consider the phrase "the people."

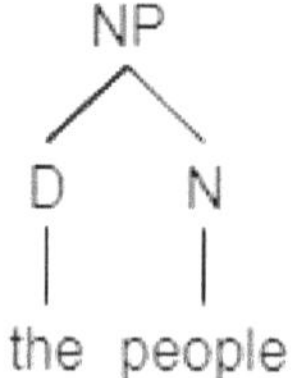

If 'people' is the head and everything else constitutes a phrase, the question arises if 'the' is a phrase. This problem disappears when NP becomes DP (Determiner Phrase) and D is the head, as shown in the following diagram.

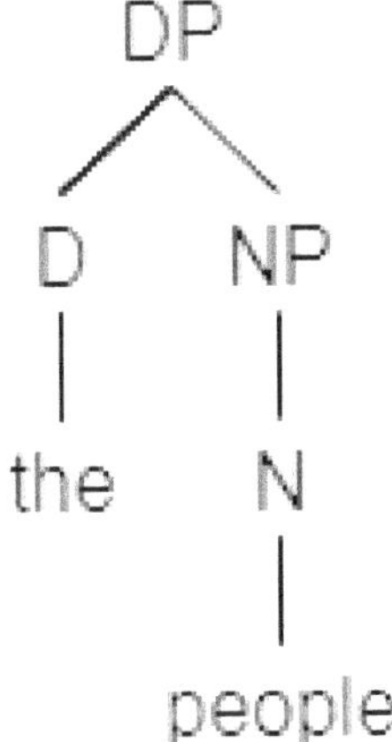

Two determiners never sit together in a phrase

*a the boy

* the these mangoes

This can be considered distributional evidence to say that the determiner is the head of the phrase.

1. A cow gives milk.
2. Each boy has a cap.
3. All girls are not dancers.

The sentences show the determiners, not nouns, and project the phrases' properties (here, agreement). It is also an excellent reason to say that D is the head of DP since the head determines the properties of the phrase.

The following evidence suggests that D is the head of the phrase: S-genitive. Previously, it was considered a morphological suffix in structures like 'John's bicycle', but later, it was realised that it is a determiner.

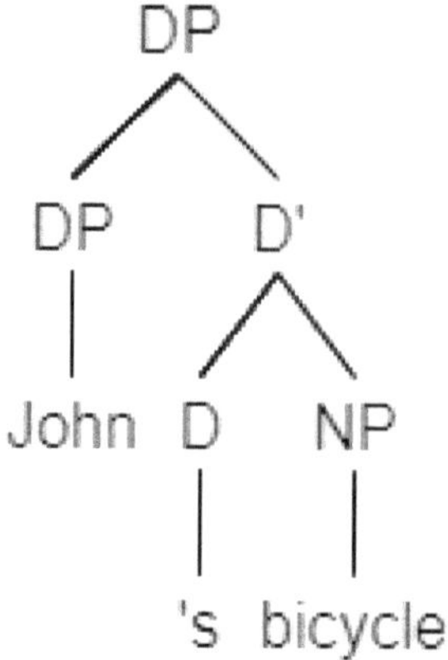

"s' is a separate entity, showing its place between possessor (John) and possessed(bicycle). If it is a suffix of John, the structure like "the boy came from town's bicycle" is impossible.

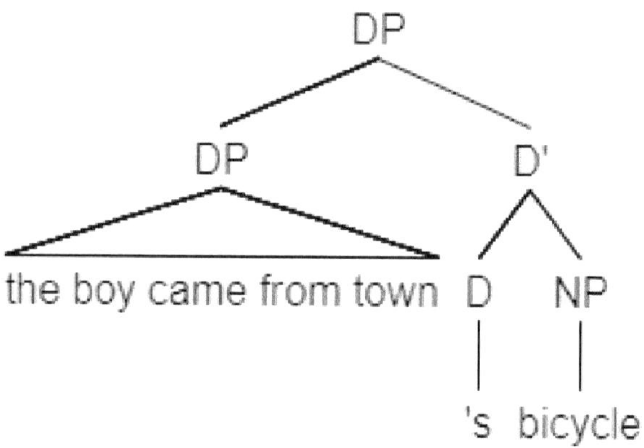

Here, "s' is related to John even though it follows town. This example also reveals that 's' is not a suffix morpheme but an independent entity.

The above arguments substantiate the idea that the determiner does not occupy the position of a modifier in an NP. Still, it is the head of a DP where the NP sits in a complement position.

Functions and distinctions of specifiers complement and adjuncts.

X-Bar schema is mainly notable for the universal structure of each phrase category. The structural pattern maintains the core word as its head, and others, such as specifier, complement and adjunct, modify it. The clear distinction of constituents and identical distribution patterns help to understand and parse the sentence more easily. This structural uniqueness makes the universality of language a strong argument.

1. Specifiers

Specifiers provide additional, often essential, information about the head and usually appear in the specifier position of a phrase, which is immediately outside the X-bar (X') in the phrase structure (XP).

Function: Specifiers typically modify or quantitatively detail the head, giving information such as quantity, definiteness, or possession. Examples include determiners in noun phrases (e.g., "the," "a"), possessive pronouns (e.g., "my," "his"), and frequency adverbs in verb phrases (e.g., "often," "always").

Placement: In the phrase structure, specifiers occupy the position just outside the X-bar level:

- NP (Noun Phrase) -> [Specifier] + N'
- VP (Verb Phrase) -> [Specifier] + V' (though less common in English)

Example: In the noun phrase "the red car," "the" is the specifier that provides definiteness to the noun "car."

2. Adjuncts

Adjuncts are optional elements that provide additional descriptive or manner information, qualifying or modifying the head without directly completing its meaning. Adjuncts can be recursive, meaning more than one adjunct can modify the same head.

Function: Adjuncts typically add descriptive information or details about circumstances (such as time, manner, and place). They do not change the essential argument structure of the head.

Placement: Adjuncts can attach either at the X-bar level (X') or the phrase level (XP), depending on the adjunct type and the structure it modifies:

- Adjuncts in VP: "She sang beautifully" (where "beautifully" modifies how "she sang")
- Adjuncts in NP: "The quickly rotating blades" (where "quickly rotating" modifies "blades")

Example: In the verb phrase "John eats quietly in the kitchen," both "quietly" (manner) and "in the kitchen" (place) are adjuncts modifying the verb phrase.

3. Complements

Complements are constituents that complete the meaning of the head by providing necessary argument structure elements. These are typically seen as mandatory to complete the function of the head in a clause or phrase.

Function: Complements fill the obligatory argument slots required by verbs, nouns, or adjectives. For example, verbs may require object complements, and prepositions require noun phrase complements.

Placement: Complements are generally placed within the X-bar (X') directly with the head:

- VP -> V' (V + [Direct Object, Indirect Object, Prepositional Phrase, etc.])
- NP -> N' (N + [Prepositional Phrase as Complement])

Example: In "She gave John a book," "John" and "a book" are complements of the verb "gave," filling the roles of indirect and direct objects, respectively.

Movements within X-bar Theory

Movement in X-bar theory primarily refers to transformations that shift constituents from their original position for various syntactic reasons:

- Wh-movement: Moves question words or phrases to the front of the sentence (e.g., "What did you eat?" where "what" moves to the sentence-initial position).
- Head Movement: A verb may move to a higher functional head for tense or agreement marking (common in many languages, like the movement from V to T in French).
- NP-movement: Often used to explain passive constructions, where the object of a verb moves to the subject position (e.g., "A book was given to John").

These movements help linguists explain various syntactic phenomena, including question formation, passive voice, and agreement. Understanding the roles and typical placements of specifiers, adjuncts, and complements is key to analysing these movements within sentences according to X-bar theory.

Head-to-head movements

Head-to-head movement in X-bar theory is crucial for explaining syntactic phenomena across languages, including English and languages like Hindi, Telugu, and Tamil. Each language demonstrates unique instances of this movement based on its specific grammatical structure. Here are examples from English and Hindi to illustrate how head-to-head movement operates in these languages.

English Examples

In English, the most common type of head-to-head movement involves moving auxiliary verbs or modals to a higher position in the clause, typically to form questions or emphasise negation.

1. Formation of Questions (V-to-T-to-C Movement)

Statement: "He is going."

Question: "Is he going?"

In the question form, the auxiliary verb "is" moves from its original position in the verb phrase (VP) to a higher tense position (T) and then to the complementiser position (C) to form a yes/no question.

2. Emphasis and Negation (T-to-C Movement)

Statement: "He has never been so happy."

Emphatic Negation: "Never has he been so happy."

Here, the auxiliary "has" moves to a higher position to accommodate the negation and emphasis, reordering the typical sentence structure for stylistic effect.

Hindi Examples

Hindi, an Indo-Aryan language, uses head-to-head movement predominantly with verbs to form questions, emphatics, and other structures. Hindi typically follows a Subject-Object-Verb (SOV) order, but movement can alter this order for specific syntactic needs.

1. Formation of Questions (V-to-T Movement)

Statement: "वह जा रहा है।" (Vah jā rahā hai) - "He is going."

Question: "क्या वह जा रहा है?" (Kyā vah jā rahā hai?) - "Is he going?"

In the question, "क्या" (kyā) is used as a question particle that often appears at the beginning of the sentence. Still, the verb "जा रहा है" (jā rahā hai) remains in its position, indicating that while the particle moves, the verb structure remains intact. Still, the sentence structure shifts to accommodate the interrogative format.

2. Politeness or Formal Emphasis (V-to-T Movement)

Formal Statement: "आप कहाँ जा रहे हैं?" (Āp kahāṁ jā rahe hain?) - "Where are you going?"

In formal or polite questions, the verb "जा रहे हैं" (jā rahe hain) remains in the verb-final position. Still, the overall structure is adjusted to accommodate formal speech, showing less explicit head movement but a shift in the syntactic structure for formality.

Telugu Example

Telugu, a Dravidian language, also exhibits verb movements primarily in questions or other syntactic constructions, following an SOV order like Hindi.

Statement: "అతను పుస్తకం చదువుతున్నాడు." (Athanu pustakam chaduvutunnādu) - "He is reading a book."

Question: "అతను పుస్తకం చదువుతున్నాడా?" (Athanu pustakam chaduvutunnādā?) - "Is he reading a book?"

In the question form, the particle "ఆ" (ā) added at the end of the verb phrase indicates a yes/no question, showing how syntactic markers move or modify the verb to form questions.

These examples illustrate that while the principle of head-to-head movement is theoretically similar across languages, its actual implementation can vary significantly depending on each language's structural and grammatical rules.

(Movements of the constituents will be discussed in detail in the chapter Movements)

Syntactic and Semantic relationships and X-Bar theory

X-bar theory, initially developed as a part of syntactic analysis within the generative grammar framework, primarily focuses on the structural organisation of phrases and sentences. Of course, X-bar theory is not a solution for resolving the semantic relationships of phrases in a sentence, but it lays the foundation for addressing the issues

Understanding Semantic and Thematic Relationships

The structured syntax approach of X-bar theory assists linguists in identifying the roles of different constituents in a sentence, which is crucial for semantic interpretation. X-bar theory makes it easier to comprehend how heads, specifiers, complements, and adjuncts interact to convey meaning by delineating the hierarchy of heads, specifiers, complements, and adjuncts.

1. Role of Specifiers and Complements:

- ➢ Specifiers often set the scope or focus of a phrase, which is crucial in interpreting quantifiers, definiteness, and possessiveness, impacting the semantic interpretation of the phrase.

- Complements complete the meaning of the head and establish necessary relationships for verbs (like objects), prepositions (objects of prepositions), and adjectives (complement clauses), which are key to understanding predicate-argument structures and thematic roles such as agent, patient, instrument, etc.

2. Role of Adjuncts:

- Adjuncts enhance the semantic richness of sentences by adding contextual information (such as manner, location, and time) without changing the core argument structure necessary for basic semantic interpretation.

Paving the Way for Government and Binding Theory

In the coming pages, we will see that the X-bar theory is not a panacea for solving all problems regarding structural relationships and semantic issues. However, the X-bar theory laid crucial groundwork for the development of the Government and Binding (GB) theory, which further refined the understanding of syntactic structures and introduced broader concepts related to syntactic dependencies.

1. Structure and Rules

The X-bar theory offered a well-structured framework for syntactic structure. The next stage of its development in Generative Grammar became the Government and Binding theory. These linguistic frameworks addressed an array of syntactic occurrences through interconnected sub-theories, such as Case theory, binding theory, and control theory.

2. Modular Grammar and Universal Design

Government and Binding theory expanded upon the modular design of X-bar theory by initiating independent yet related modules of syntax that interact based on principles of modularity. This methodology permitted a deeper examination of linguistic phenomena across languages, emphasising universally the architectural foundations of syntax.

3. Government

In GB theory, government encompasses the relationship between a governing word (typically a verb or preposition) and its dependents. Comprehending syntactic processes, such as the assignment of case to noun phrases and certain rules of movement within the syntax, requires this relationship.

4. Binding

Binding theory deals with the interpretation of pronouns and other noun phrases in relation to one another in sentences. This helped not only to address the unclear area of understanding pronouns but also to define the semantic issues in the sentence.

X-bar theory impacted Government and Binding theory by moving from exclusively syntactic structures to an integrated approach that also considers how these structures affect the syntactic and semantic characteristics of sentences. The transition had a significant impact on theoretical linguistics, offering more profound insights into the syntax-semantics interface and enhancing our understanding of language structure and function. We will discuss all these in detail in the chapter 'Principles and Parameters'.

Cross-linguistic applications of X-bar theory

The history of Generative Grammar states that the emergence of X-Bar theory was due to the necessity of resolving many issues that PSG and TGG were incapable of answering. The primary issue was that neither of the previous versions could provide a consistent structure for phrases, as per the assertion that GG stands for universal grammar. The X-bar theory has been successful in delivering a universal structure that is suitable for all phrases that comprise a head, followed by complements and preceded by specifiers. This enhanced the possibility of cross-linguistic application of X-bar theory to compare and contrast the syntactic structures of languages as diverse as English and various Indian languages, such as Hindi, Tamil, Telugu, Malayalam, etc.

Universal Structure in X-bar Theory

Phrasal Categories: Across languages, phrases can be broken down into noun phrases (NP), verb phrases (VP), adjective phrases (AdjP), and prepositional phrases (PP), each structured around a central head.

Hierarchical Levels: Each phrase can be analysed at different levels: the head level (X), the intermediate level (X'), and the phrasal level (XP). This hierarchical organisation helps in understanding how different syntactic elements are grouped and function within sentences.

Examples in English and Indian Languages

1. **Noun Phrases (NP)**

English: In the NP "the beautiful garden," "garden" is the noun head, "beautiful" is an adjective modifying the noun, and "the" is a specifier determining the noun.

Hindi: In a Hindi NP, "वह सुंदर बगीचा" (vah sundar bagīcā, "that beautiful garden"), "बगीचा" (bagīcā, "garden") is the head, "सुंदर" (sundar, "beautiful") serves as an adjective, and "वह" (vah, "that") is the specifier.

2. Verb Phrases (VP)

English: In the VP “will read the book,” “read” is the verb head, “the book” is the object complement, and “will” is an auxiliary verb modifying the tense of the main verb.

Tamil: In a Tamil VP “புத்தகத்தை வாசிப்பார்” (puththakaththai vāsippār, “will read the book”), “வாசிப்பார்” (vāsippār, “will read”) is the head, and “புத்தகத்தை” (puththakaththai, “the book”) is the object complement. Tamil often uses postpositions instead of prepositions, showing the flexibility of X-bar theory in adapting to different syntactic typologies.

3. Adjective Phrases (AdjP)

English: In “very beautiful,” “beautiful” is the adjective head, and “very” is an adverb modifying the adjective.

Telugu: In a Telugu AdjP “చాలా అందంగా” (chālā andaṅgā, “very beautiful”), “అందంగా” (andaṅgā, “beautiful”) is the adjective head, and “చాలా” (chālā, “very”) is an adverb modifying the adjective.

Cross-Linguistic Applications.

- Syntactic Analysis: X-bar theory allows for the consistent examination of sentence construction across languages by giving structure to syntactic examination, regardless of language-specific rules.
- Language Comparison: With a shared framework, linguists can directly match how different languages arrange similar syntactic aspects, exposing underlying commonalities and one-of-a-kind qualities.
- Theoretical Linguistics: Insights gained from applying X-bar theory cross-linguistically feed into broader theoretical

discussions about the structure of language, influencing theories of syntax and grammar.

- Implications for Understanding Language Universals: The cross-linguistic relevance of X-bar theory underscores potential syntactical principles shared across all languages. It suggests that despite superficial dissimilarities, languages exhibit common underlying structures in how they form phrases and sentences. This common ground aids in developing computational models for natural language processing and enhances our comprehension of human language.

Synopsis of the Chapter

X-bar theory is a foundational framework in syntax within Generative Grammar that introduces a universal, hierarchical structure for all phrases. It addresses the limitations of traditional Transformational Generative Grammar (TGG) and phrase structure rules (PSRs) by establishing a uniform, binary branching structure for syntactic representation. This theory not only addresses inconsistencies in TGG but also establishes the foundation for further developments in syntax, including Principles and Parameters Theory, Binding Principles Theory, the DP Hypothesis, and CP clauses.

1. Identical Structure of Binary Branching

- Universal Structure: X-bar theory posits that all phrases—whether noun phrases (NP), verb phrases (VP), adjective phrases (AdjP), etc.—have the same basic hierarchical structure:
- Binary Branching: Enforces a consistent two-branch structure at every level, eliminating flat or non-binary structures present in earlier models of TGG.

Advantages:

1. Cross-Linguistic Consistency: Explains why all languages share a similar underlying syntactic structure despite surface-level differences (e.g., SVO vs. SOV languages).
2. Reduced Reliance on Transformations: Instead of relying on complex transformational rules, X-bar theory builds sentences incrementally in a systematic, hierarchical manner.
3. Modularity: Each phrase is composed of heads, complements, specifiers, and adjuncts in predictable configurations, making syntactic structures easier to analyse.

2. Resolving Issues in Phrase Structure Rules (PSRs) and TGG

- Uniform Representation: Earlier PSRs were language-specific and varied greatly. X-bar theory standardises the representation of phrases across languages.
- Recursion and Hierarchy: Explains recursion (e.g., embedding one phrase within another) more naturally by allowing recursive projections.
- Head-Complement Relation: Clarifies the syntactic relationship between a head (e.g., N, V, P) and its complement.

3. Connection to Principles and Parameters Theory

- Principles: Universal rules that apply to all languages, such as the binary branching structure and head-complement relationships.
- Parameters: Language-specific variations, such as head-initial (e.g., English) vs. head-final (e.g., Japanese) structures.
- Impact: X-bar theory provided the formalism needed to articulate principles and parameters, enabling a deeper understanding of cross-linguistic variation.

4. Contribution to Binding Principles

- Binding Theory: Explains the relationships between pronouns, reflexives, and their antecedents.
- Example: "John saw himself" (reflexive pronoun) vs. "John saw him" (regular pronoun).
- X-bar Theory's Role: The hierarchical structure of phrases helps define c-command, a critical concept in binding theory, where a node governs or commands another node in the tree.

5. The DP Hypothesis

- Proposes that noun phrases (NPs) are dominated by a determiner phrase (DP), making the determiner (e.g., "the," "a") the head of the phrase.
- Example: "The big dog"
- DP → D' → D (the) + NP (big dog).
- Impact: Highlights the functional structure of phrases and aligns noun phrases with the structural patterns seen in verb and adjective phrases.

6. CP Clauses

- Proposes that complementiser phrases (CPs) dominate sentences and clauses, with the complementiser (e.g., "that," "if") as the head of the phrase.
- Example: "John said [that Mary is happy]"
- CP → C' → C (that) + TP (Mary is happy).
- Significance: Explains clause embedding, question formation, and movement (e.g., wh-movement).

Conclusion

Syntactic analysis was transformed by the X-bar theory's introduction of a universal hierarchical structure for phrases, which addressed inconsistencies in phrase structure rules and TGG. It laid the foundation for the creation of Principles and Parameters Theory, Binding Theory, and the exploration of functional categories like DPs and CPs. The study of syntax and linguistic universals is anchored by the X-bar theory's establishment of binary branching and modularity.

CHAPTER IV

INFLECTIONAL PHRASE (IP)

Assuming that the entire sentence is a phrase, if we consider the structure of the sentence, the verb would be the proposed head of the sentence. But, to the question, what truly makes a verb a verb is its ability to inflection. This makes the inflectional element the head of the sentence, from where it is named as the Inflectional Phrase (IP), also referred as Tense Phrase (TP).

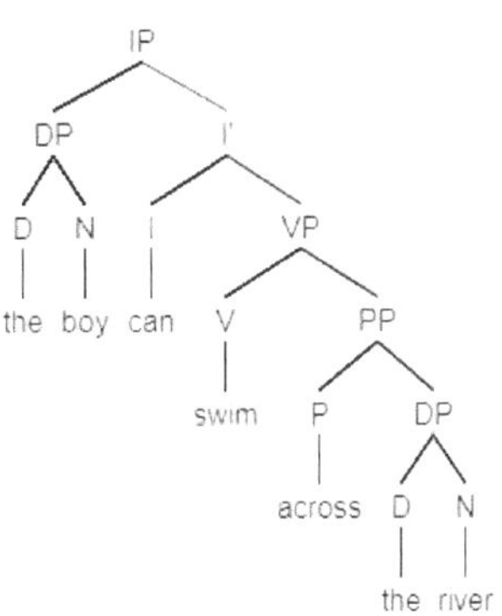

The boy can swim across the river.

While this sounds convenient and reasonable, it is not beyond raising a few issues. The first is why the inflectional node is the head, not the verb. The hypothesis is that the verb does not project as the head in a sentence as it does not decide the properties of the whole sentence. Properties such as tense, gender, plurality, case, aspect, and mode of the sentence have nothing to do with the verb, but auxiliaries or modals project all these. So, the only remaining option is for the modals and auxiliaries to be the head of the sentence. Here comes the following issue: Why is the DP in the diagram tree above in the position of the specifier when it ought to be in the specifier of the verb?

The magician may reveal the secrets today.

We saw earlier that some movements of the components are possible within a sentence. If we pick up the sentence above,

Today, the magician may reveal the secrets.

These all are possible movements in the sentence without creating any ungrammaticalities. Thus, the answer to why the DP becomes the specifier of the inflectional verb rather than the main verb is due to movements.

The diagram below shows how the movement took place.

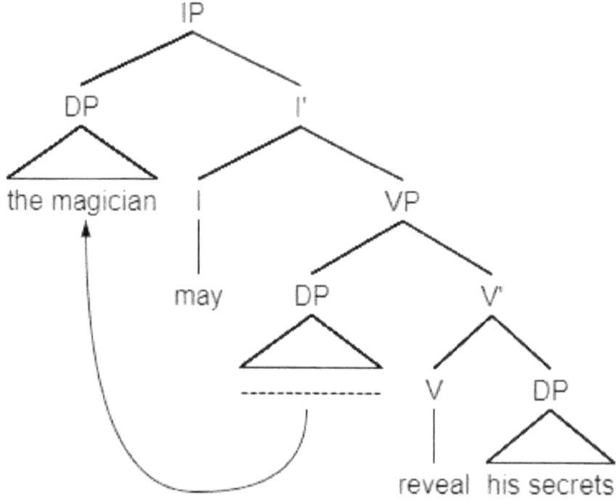

The solution for problems related to the negation of the phrase may also add a branch to the I bar.

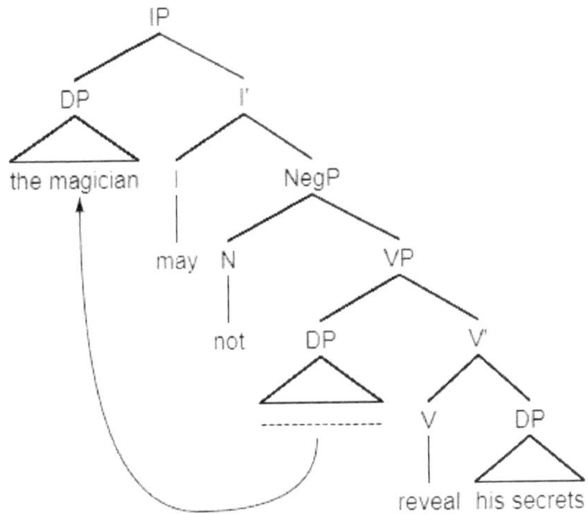

Thus, leaving an empty node may explain how the specifier position of the specifier DP is an argument of the Inflectional node.

When we need to add a modifier, it will take the adjunct position. The particularity of the adjunct node is that it would be a daughter to a bar node and a sister to another. In addition to that, adjuncts are recursive.

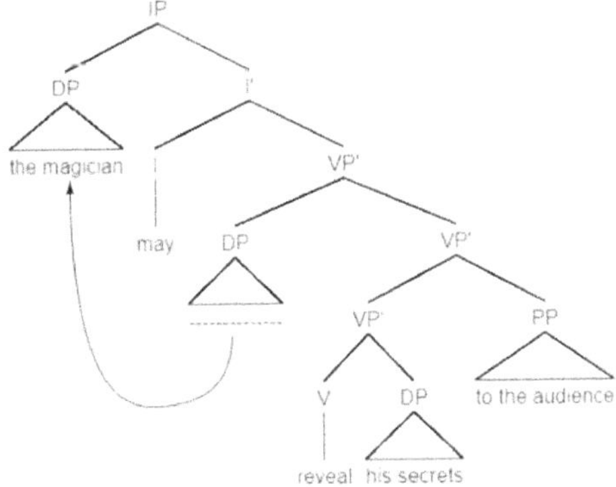

If more adjuncts are necessary, the VP would be multiplied, satisfying the only condition that its mother node and sister node should be bar nodes.

More discussion is needed regarding movements, and we will do so in the coming pages.

Now, let us see how the IP structure helps to identify and build different types of clauses or CPs (Complementiser Phrases) in sentences. Before this, we will discuss some other categories of verbs we have not yet encountered.

LIGHT VERBS

Light verbs have little to do with the semantic content of a sentence, but they do exist as parsing agents. Delexical verbs are also called because they do not individually contribute to the sentence's meaning. The verbs used in this context are do, give, get, have, let, make, and take. Note that auxiliaries are also delexical in that they do not make sense but are not light verbs because they do not match other criteria.

a. Mother gave her child a bath.
b. The child made the mud pot break.
c. He did the review of the film.
d. The statement got severe criticism.
e. We had a talk.

The above sentences are examples of light verbs. They mean that

a. the Mother bathed the child
b. The child broke the mud pot.
c. He reviewed the film.
d. The statement was severely criticised.
e. We talked.

The comparison shows that even though the light verbs are delexical, they successfully distribute the theta roles, which are a lexical property of lexical verbs.

UNACCUSATIVE VERBS

Typically, an agent or experiencer takes the position of DP specifier of a VP or verb, whereas an Unaccusative verb takes a theme or a patient as a specifier. In other words, a simple phrase construction with a theme or a patient as a subject and a verb is an example of the verb Unaccusative.

1. The train departed.
2. A letter arrived.
3. The dog died.
4. The mist disappeared.
5. The disease spread.

To a certain extent, Unaccusative verbs are intransitive, but simultaneously they are different. The distinguishing features of an Unaccusative verb are 1) 'there' subject construction is possible, 2) the inversion of the locative PPs can be possible, and 3) an Unaccusative verb does not take any types of objects as its complement

For example,

1. There departed the train.
2. There arrived the letter.
3. There died the dog.
4. There disappeared the mist.
5. There spread disease.

An example of PP inversion is as follows,

There arrived a letter from my friend.

From my friend there arrived a letter.

It will be clearer if we compare this with an ordinary intransitive verb.

The girl smiled.

*there smiled the girl. (Ungrammatical; it is a customary way in Generative Grammar to mark a sentence with an asterisk to show the sentence is either ungrammatical or unacceptable.)

*In the garden smiled the girl. (ungrammatical)

The girl smiled an artful smile. (Thus, the intransitive verb can rarely have an object, unlike the Unaccusative verb.)

ERGATIVE VERBS

1. The glasses shattered.
2. The tree grew.
3. His career ended.
4. The window closed.
5. The heads rolled.

If we compare the verbs in the examples above with Unaccusative verbs, we will see the non-agentive or patient theme as a subject. However, the resemblance ends here. In contrast to Unaccusative verbs, these verbs have a transitive context of usage, such as.

1. I shattered the glasses.
2. The gardener grew the trees.

3. He ended his career.
4. She closed the window.
5. The king rolled the heads.

Note that these verbs may not be used as *their* subject context.

*there shattered I the glasses

*There ended he his career.

They will eventually result in ungrammatical entities.

Reversing the PP is also not possible for such sentences.

*in the room shattered I glasses.

*Within one year ended he his career.

So, the verbs with transitive and Unaccusative usage are called Ergative Verbs.

IP AND LIGHT VERB, ETC.

In generative grammar, particularly within the framework of X-bar theory and its developments like Government and Binding and Minimalist Program, verbs play a central role in the formation and interpretation of sentence structures. We have already observed how a verb can behave, and now we want to discuss how light verbs behave differently, particularly in an IP phrase paradigm. As we progress to more advanced concepts like GB theory and the minimalist approach, this understanding will become more crucial. At the moment, we are examining the standard analysis of these types of verbs.

1. Light Verbs

Light verbs have little semantic content on their own and are used primarily to help form verb phrases, often in combination with another noun or adjective that carries the main semantic load.

- IP Interaction: In IP structures, light verbs often merge with their complements to form a predicate. They are crucial in projecting the IP because they help carry the inflectional properties (like tense, aspect, and mood) necessary for the sentence to be grammatically correct.
- Example: In a sentence like "She gave a smile," "gave" is a light verb that combines with "a smile" to form a verb phrase. The light verb "gave" carries tense information and assists in forming the predicate.

2. Unaccusative Verbs

These verbs are more or less intransitive verbs, but there is a difference in that an intransitive verb takes an Agent as the subject, but an Unaccusative verb takes an object (a patient or theme) as its subject. So, this affects the argument structure of the sentence, especially in terms of the allotment of cases and thematic roles. (We will discuss the concept of Agent, Patient, Theme Goal, etc., in the chapter Principles and Parameters in more detail.)

IP Interaction: In generative grammar, Unaccusative verbs are seen as having their subjects originate in the object position within VP (Verb Phrase) and then move to the subject position of the IP for syntactic reasons, such as satisfying case requirements.

- Example: In the sentence "The glass broke," "broke" is an Unaccusative verb. The subject, "the glass," is not performing the action but is being affected by it, indicating a movement from an underlying object position to the subject position in IP.

3. Ergative Verbs

Ergative verbs, or verbs that exhibit ergative behaviour, are those where the subject of an intransitive verb is treated like the object of a transitive verb. This behaviour is especially notable in ergative languages, but elements of it can be observed in the syntactic structure of languages that aren't typically ergative.

- IP Interaction: In terms of IP structures, the treatment of subjects in sentences with ergative verbs can vary. In languages with ergative-absolutive alignment, the subject of an ergative verb (agent) may not necessarily move to the typical subject position within IP as it would in nominative-accusative languages.
- Example: In a theoretical English ergative structure, you might analyse "He cooked" and "The soup cooked" differently. In "He cooked," "he" functions as an agent and would be in the typical subject position. In "The soup cooked," "the soup" behaves more like a patient undergoing the action, which might imply a different syntactic treatment, though English does not fully display ergative syntax.

General Considerations in IP Structures

- In IP structure, the inflectional elements within the sentence are a point of interaction for a verb. In other words, inflectional properties, which are mainly carried by modals and auxiliaries, are responsible for determining plurality, tense aspects, and other aspects.
- Movement and Syntax: The movement of subjects or objects in relation to IP is often dictated by the verb type, which influences how thematic roles are assigned and how arguments are structured within the sentence.

The analysis of these verb types within IP structures is fundamental in generative grammar because it helps linguists understand deeper aspects of language, such as how different verbs dictate the syntactic structure and interpretation of sentences, how arguments are introduced and moved in syntax, and how these movements affect the overall semantic interpretation of sentences.

CP PHRASES

Phrases held together by a complementiser are generally called Complementiser Phrases (CPs), which may or may not be finite. Complementisers belong to the functional category.

John said that he would start a new business.

In this sentence, 'that he would start a new business' is a CP clause and 'that' is a complementiser. The primary analysis shows that the clause is an IP introduced by the complementiser. The IP and the complementiser form a constituent of the whole sentence. Evidence that the clause is a constituent is that it may be substituted with a pronoun or that a similar clause may be coordinated.

I thought he bought a new car.

We can also present the CP Clause omitting the complementiser 'that'. It shows that the complementiser is not obligatory for the clauses introduced by the 'that' category. Here, we must understand that though the complementiser is not present, an empty node will represent the same in the Deep Structure.

Babu wondered if John would start a new business.

The complementiser should not be omitted in the above sentence, as doing so deletes the clause's very nature.

If we apply the X'-schema, the structure of a CP clause is as follows (C represents the complementiser)

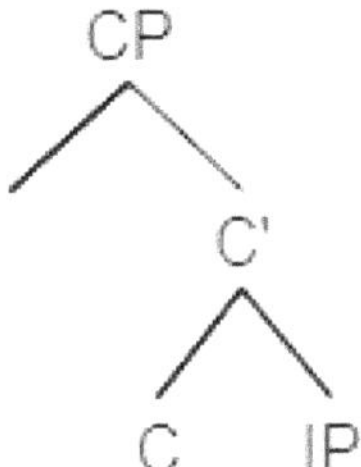

This diagram shows that IP is the complement of the complementiser, and the C' is the sister node to the specifier node of the maximal projection CP.

Let us see the diagram for the sentence.

Babu said that he had already written a novel.

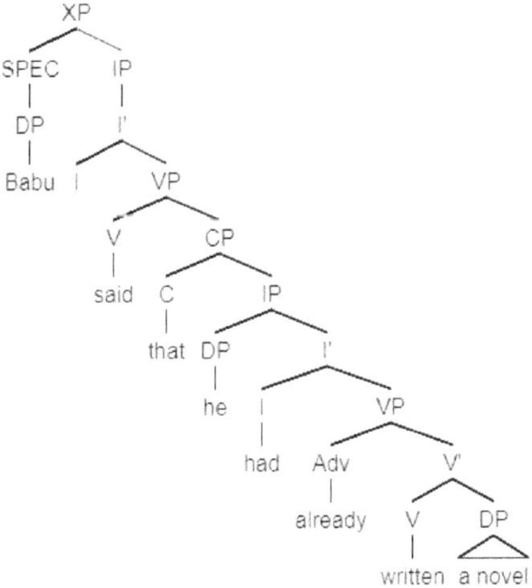

It seems to be all right, but sometimes the XP or main clause becomes CP (embedded clause) of a sentence like;

Raju told me that Babu said he had already written a novel.

XP
SPEC CP
SPEC C'
C IP
DP I'
Raju I VP
V'
V DP
told me CP
SPEC C'
C IP
that DP VP
Babu V CP
said (that)he had already written a novel.

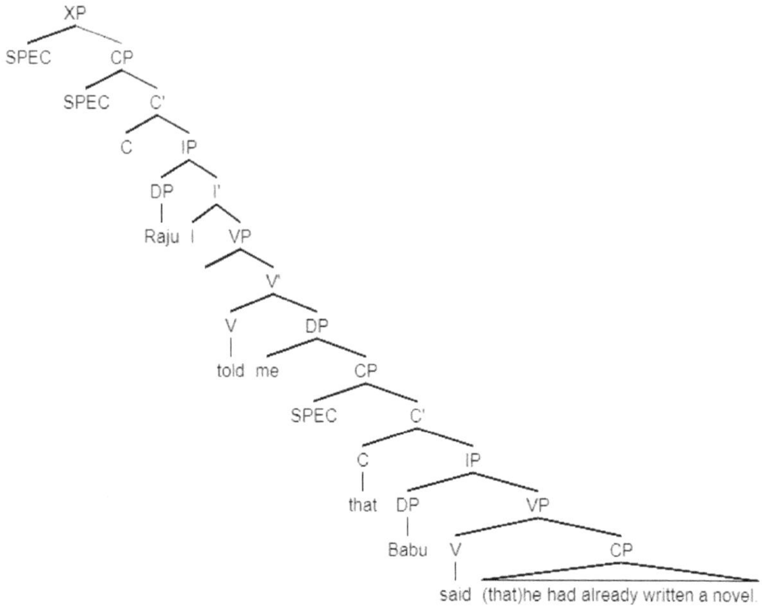

The diagram shows that each clause structure belongs to another clause, as the clauses are recursive.

To say this briefly, a typical sentence structure may be shown below.

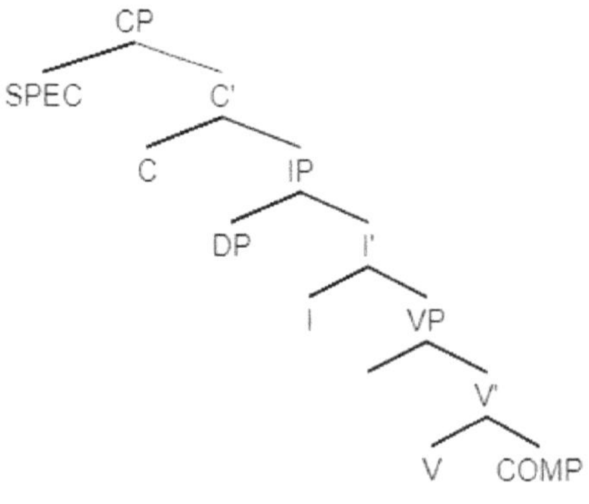

CP
SPEC C'
C IP
DP I'
I VP
V'
V COMP

1. The boy said that his girlfriend was a dancer.

We already knew that the sentence has two clauses and the structure of both.

First clause

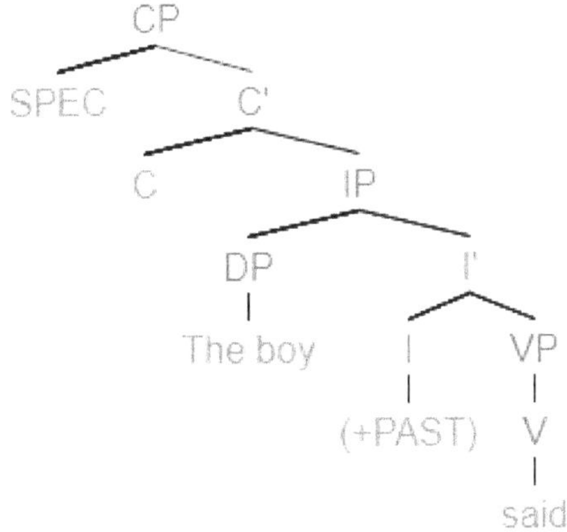

Clause 2

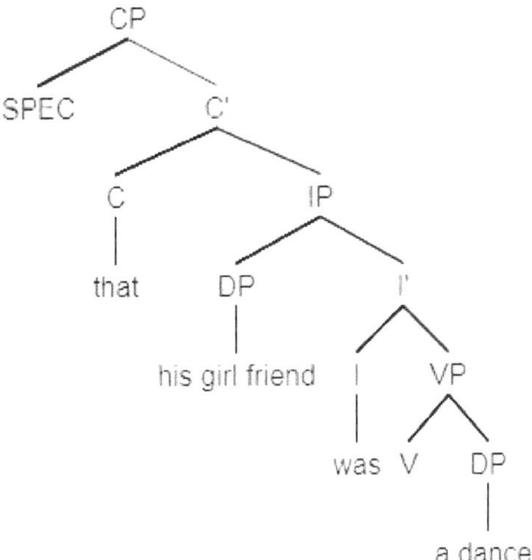

What remains is to join them to get the whole sentence.

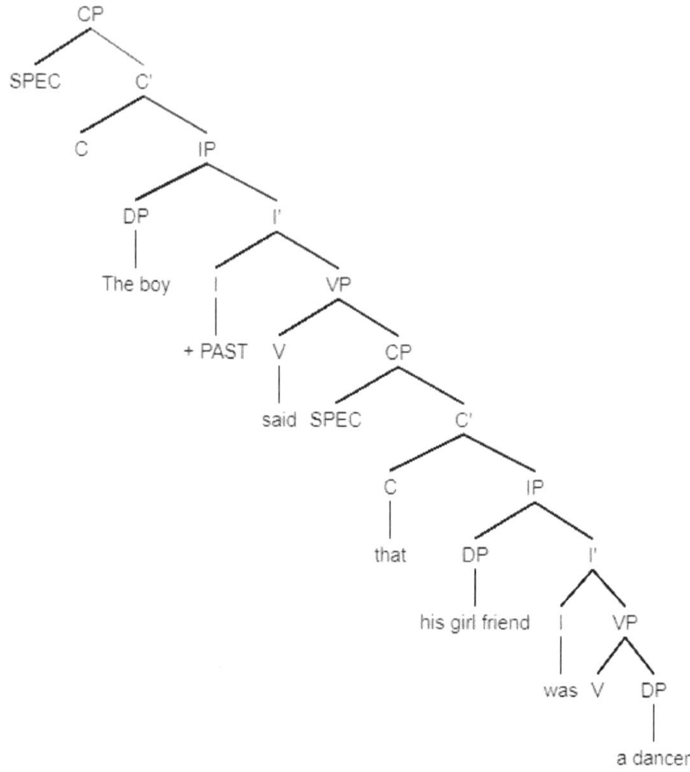

The syntactical construction of the complementiser clauses (CP) of which "if/whether" is the complementiser is the same as that of "that" as the complementiser. The only difference in this respect is that 'whether/if' is mandatory in the first case, and 'that' is optional in the second.

Before proceeding to other CP clauses, such as relative clauses, we need to discuss the movements of "wh"-question words to understand them better. We have already discussed in a previous chapter that specific movements of words take place to form a question. Here, we will discuss the same to understand why and how the movements occurred.

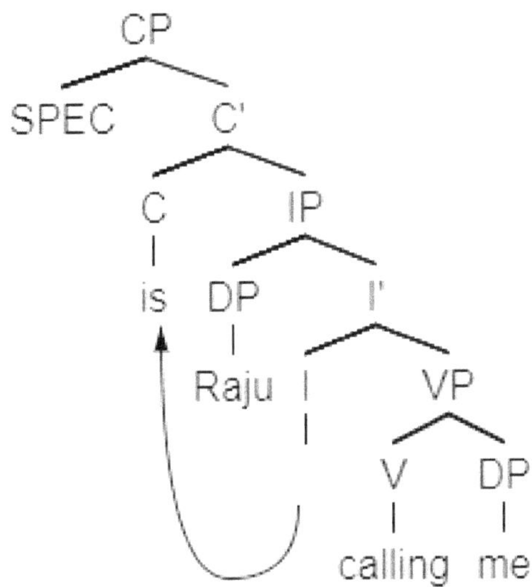

The auxiliary moved to sit in the node C (complementiser). The specific reasons for moving the auxiliary to the complement node (C) are as follows:

a. this is the closest void node in the ascending direction.
b. The complement node (C) accommodates the question element if one is in the specific language. Since there is no question element in English, auxiliaries take its position.

Then comes the question of the wh-word, its movements and which node a wh-word moves to.

Raju is talking with Rahim.

Let us make an echo question replacing Rahim with who as "Raju is talking with who?

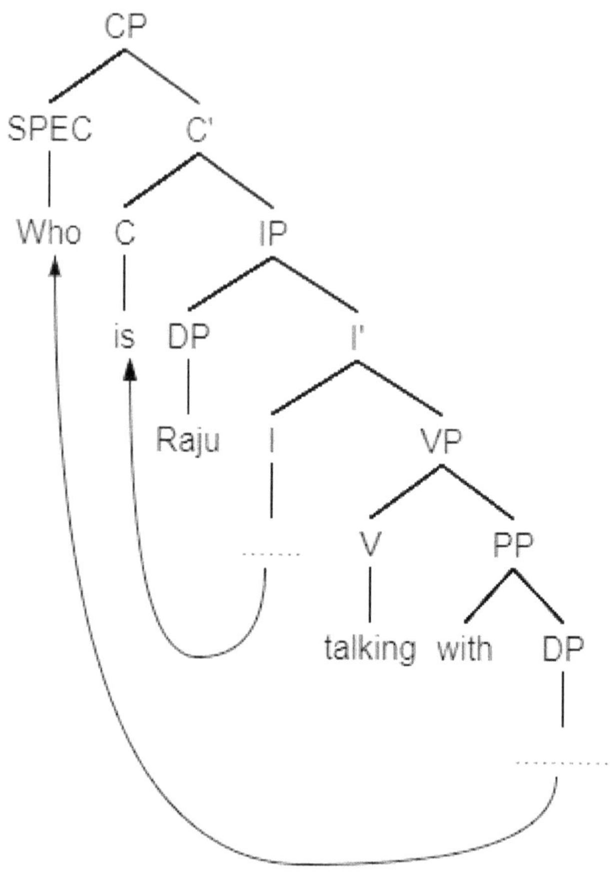

This shows the position of "who" is a DP. When the echo question is turned to the real question, the wh-word moves away from there to the SPEC and forms a question like "Who is Raju talking with?"

It is important to remember that the inversion of the auxiliary does not occur when the question is embedded. It is also worth noting that the complementiser in the embedded clause sat on SPEC rather than on the 'C' node.

Ex: The teacher asked why the boy did not complete the project.

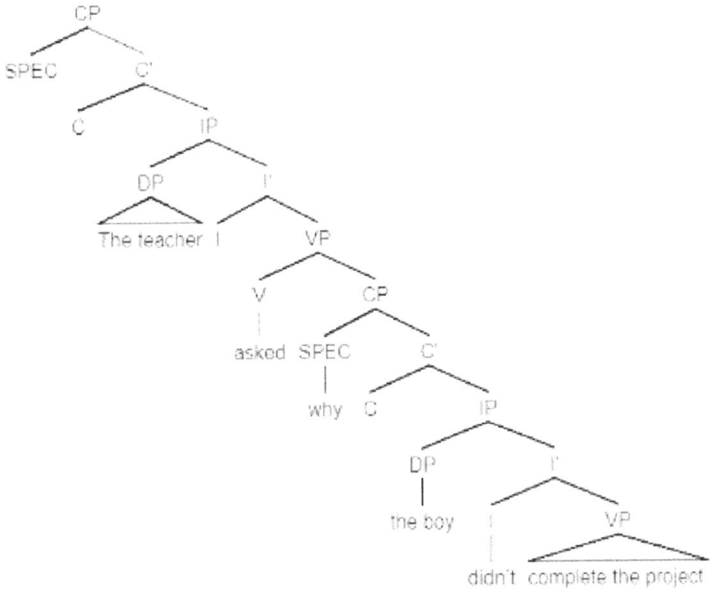

Movements of wh-words greatly influence syntactic structure; we must discuss them later.

Synopsis of the Chapter

The concept of the Inflectional Phrase (IP) is a significant advancement in generative grammar that treats sentences as hierarchical structures dominated by an inflectional element. The core concept behind an Inflectional phrase (IP) is that the verb's inflectional properties make it the focal point of the sentence. If we go deeper into the concept, we will see that inflectional elements are mostly additions to verbs, such as modals and auxiliaries, as they determine main functions such as agreement, aspect, and tense. The XP (Maximum Projection of the sentence) is what the inflectional element represents, which is why we refer to the sentence as an

IP clause. When a complementiser and an IP are combined, a Complementiser Phrase (CP) is created, and each IP can be a part of a CP that is positioned at a higher level of IP.

1. Sentence as an Inflectional Phrase

- Definition: A sentence is represented as an Inflectional Phrase (IP), where the Inflection (I) head governs the structure and integrates grammatical features such as tense, mood, and agreement.
- Structure:
- IP→SPEC+I'
- I'→I+VP

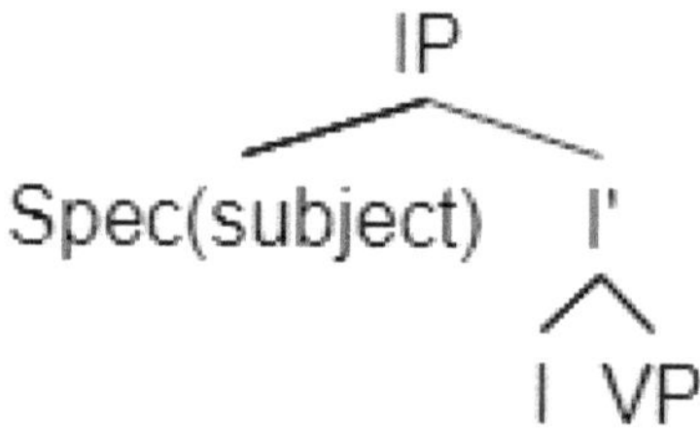

- Significance: The sentence becomes IP where 'I' takes the central position as Head of it, determining the whole properties.
- The subject occupies the specifier lot to fulfil the requirement of the Extended Projection Principle, which requires that there must be a subject in a non-pro-drop language like English. (This point will be further elaborated in the future.)

2. Modals and Auxiliaries to decide the nature of the IP.

- Role of Modals and Auxiliaries:
- Modals (e.g., "can," "must") and auxiliaries (e.g., "have," "be") appear in the I-head position and define the sentence's grammatical nature (e.g., tense, aspect, mood).

- Example:
- "John will eat" (future tense)
- "John has eaten" (perfect aspect)
- Contrast with Main Verbs:
- Main verbs appear in the VP and depend on modals/auxiliaries in the I-head to express tense or aspect.
- Example: "John eats" vs. "John is eating."

3. Verb Classification and Their Impact on IP

- Light Verbs: Verbs like "do," "make," and "take" add minimal semantic content and often support grammatical functions.
- Example: "She took a walk."
- Unaccusative Verbs: Verbs whose subjects originate as internal arguments within the VP.
- Example: "The vase broke." (Subject "the vase" is initially the object of the verb.)
- Ergative verbs are verbs that can change between transitive and intransitive forms, with the object of the transitive version being the subject of the intransitive version. For example, observe the difference in the two sentences,

   i. The meal cooked
   ii. Mother cooked the meal.

The verb is used as an ergative verb in the first sentence, while the second sentence is the transitive version of the first.

Difference from Other Verbs:

- When we compare traditional transitive and intransitive verbs, we understand that these classes of verbs affect argument structure and influence IP interpretation.

4. Inflectional Phrase and CP Clauses

- IP as a Component of CP:
- CPs (Complementizer Phrases) dominate IPs in the hierarchical structure of sentences.
- Example: "John said [that Mary is happy]"
- CP → C' → C ("that") + IP ("Mary is happy").
- Role of IP in Subordinate Clauses:
- IP provides the core syntactic structure, while CP introduces complementisers (e.g., "that," "if") to connect the clause to the larger sentence.
- Wh-Movement and Modals:
- Wh-movement (e.g., "What will John eat?") relies on the interaction between the CP and the IP, where the modal or auxiliary in the I-head supports the question formation.

5. IP in Generative Grammar

- IP unifies sentence structure by providing a unified framework to analyse sentences across different languages, highlighting the importance of functional categories like tense and agreement.
- The IP paradigm highlights the dependency of verbs on inflectional elements, which helps to maintain grammatical features.
- CP and IP: the IP is the embedded part of a CP in a complex sentence, and this serves as the basis for analysing more complex syntactic structures. We will see in the future that IP and CP relations play more significant roles in advanced syntactical theories like the Government and Binding (GB) theory.

Conclusion

The concept of the Inflectional Phrase (IP) made a significant advancement in Generative Grammar as it made inflectional elements the head of the sentence. This shift of focus from verbs to inflectional elements, such as modals and auxiliaries, not only makes analysing a sentence easier but also helps to define the CP structure more rationally. The classification of verbs into light verbs, Unaccusative verbs, and ergative verbs further refines syntactic analysis. The IP framework is a valuable tool in modern syntax theory because it provides insight into clause embedding and higher-level sentence structures from the interaction between IPs and CPs.

CHAPTER V

PRINCIPLES AND PARAMETERS

It is accepted that children worldwide learn their languages rapidly, along with all sorts of grammar. The rapidity of language acquisition shows that specific accessible frameworks contribute to a child's success. Now that we have initiated the discussion in our previous chapters, it is time to examine them in detail.

The primary assessment suggests that a child has the innate ability to use Language Acquisition Devices (LAD) to learn their mother tongue during specific early childhood periods. To build up the internalised language and mental grammar, a child depends on the framework based on Principles and Parameters (P&P). To put it differently, establishing the principles and parameters of a given language makes language learning easier. When we say Principle in this context, it states something universal about language. For example, nouns have plural forms, which are indeed for all languages and all nouns. However, the morphology of plural forms may differ from noun to noun and language to language, so we call it a Parameter. In simple terms, when discussing Principles and Parameters, Principles are universal, while Parameters are language-specific.

Although sentences in a language are infinite, each does not establish a set of rules, as we have seen. All sentences are made up of a limited number of regulations. Having established this as something universal, we still use sentences as the basic unit of grammaticality. Examining a sentence's grammar before or after it is unnecessary to determine its grammatical acceptability. A native speaker's intuitiveness may quickly indicate if a sentence is ungrammatical, but his intuitive powers alone cannot establish the ungrammaticality.

We have observed that Phrase Structure Grammar (PSG), Transformational Generative Grammar (TGG) and X-bar theory are so powerful that they can over-generate sentences regardless of grammaticality. To keep track and balance, we now require a framework. The emergence of Principles and Parameters precisely meets the requirements mentioned above. Universal Grammar (UG) is a term for the characteristics that make up all languages worldwide, and the parametrised elements are either local or language-specific. For example, let us consider the structure of a sentence in any language. It may be in SOV, SVO, or VSO patterns. Here, the presence of S, V, and O (Subject, Verb, and Object) is mandatory for all languages; hence, it is universal. A parameter is a term used to describe their distribution specific to a language. It is inappropriate to leave this topic without mentioning that the Universal Grammar mentioned earlier is a genetic achievement of the human species. Regardless of their cognitive capabilities, everyone can quickly learn the language surrounding them. Mastering a second or third language is a different endeavour and a diverse topic. Even in the case of mother tongue language acquisition, it does not happen solely through learning. It depends on various factors, such as linguistic sensitivity, being under the influence of UG, being exposed to a language environment, etc. In addition, to develop language, the child must develop their mental lexicon to use words correctly.

From the beginning, by discussing theories, we aim to understand how the human mind, specifically a child's psyche, acquires language using mental grammar and the framework that supports it. We now know how groundbreaking the PSRs, TGGs, and X-Bar theories were in helping us understand them and how the constraints and limitations of each paved the way for the next. In this regard, the advent of Government and Binding (GB) theory has been so innovative that there has been a top-to-bottom affluence in Generative Grammar, both theoretically and empirically.

GOVERNMENT AND BINDING THEORY

In the 1980s, Chomsky proposed the Government and Binding (GB) theory as a model for syntax in generative grammar. The incorporation of more abstract and complex mechanisms to explain linguistic phenomena represents an evolution of earlier generative models, like the Standard Theory and Extended Standard Theory. The modular approach of GB theory involves several sub-theories or modules intertwining to account for various syntactic structures and processes. The objective of this framework is to streamline the descriptive apparatus of syntax to a more fundamental set of rules and constraints, resulting in a greater understanding of universal grammar. The GB theory is considered to be a remedial method for many limitations and restrictions of previous generative models, as well as a pioneering approach in many contexts.

Key Components of Government and Binding Theory

GB theory consists of several key components that contribute to the generative paradigm of current and future developments. We will proceed through them in a sequence.

1. We have already discussed the progress of X-bar theory and its far-reaching innovations extensively. The most important of all is the universal template for phrase structure. This establishes a uniform hierarchical organisation for phrase structure and strengthens the concept of a universal approach for all languages. Furthermore, it introduces modularity to sentence structure and establishes distributional positions for specifiers, complements, and adjuncts.
2. Theta (Θ) Theory: This theory introduces the argument structure of the constituents, which clarifies relationships and the dependency nature of different components in sentences. This is possible through the assignment of thematic roles (theta roles) to different syntactic arguments such as Agent, Patient, Theme, etc. It is also centred around the Theta Criterion, which requires each argument to bear one and only one unique thematic role and assign each thematic role to one argument.
3. Case Theory: This is all about consigning cases, such as nominative, accusative, etc., to each argument in a sentence. It also describes how syntactic cases are essential for DPs to restrict ungrammaticality in a sentence. The right case assignment is known as a Case Filter, which determines the legitimacy of a sentence
4. Binding Theory: The concept of binding theory is the explanation of how noun phrases (pronouns, anaphors, and referential expressions) are correctly or incorrectly bound in sentences. According to this theory, anaphors should be bound in their governing domain, pronominals shouldn't be bound in their governing domain, and R-expressions should be free.

5. Control Theory: This explains how non-finite clauses (such as infinitives) are determined. Control theory assists us in determining whether an infinitive clause's subject is controlled by external arguments or arbitrarily.
6. Movement Theory (Move α): This theory suggests that constituents move from one position to another within a sentence to satisfy syntactic constraints. The Move α theory asserts why and how movements take place, including head movements, wh-movements, and raising. It also explains the local conditions that restrict movement
7. Government Theory: Defines the relationships between a governing word and its dependents. It explains how certain syntactic elements (heads) affect the distribution and interpretation of others in phrases or clauses, which affects things like the proper assignment of null elements.

We will examine the theories mentioned above and related in more detail now. The focus of our discussion will be on the terms, their applicability, and how they limit ungrammaticality.

ARGUMENTS

Over and again, we have observed and stated that a sentence is not merely a string of words, though words are the building blocks. Different types of words make up the initial constituents of a sentence, which are various types of phrases. The question that arises is why and how certain word patterns occur in a sentence, whether they are chosen randomly or due to other factors.

The choice of words is often determined by the argument structure of others, not just the speaker's selection. The argument property of phrases also plays a role in deciding grammatical righteousness. An argument is the engagement of one word with another in a sentence, either by influencing or being influenced by each other to expose their true nature. It also determines the possibility of coexistence.

1. Raju slept.
2. The little girl plucked a flower.
3. Meena gave her spouse a surprise gift.
4. Asok placed the bouquet on his table.

Sentence 1 consists of two components, namely a DP (Raju) and a VP (slept). The verb slept is a one-place argument because it cannot accept another DP argument.

Sentence 2 has a subject DP (the little girl) and a predicate DP (a flower) just because the verb pluck needs at least two arguments.

In sentence three, there are three DPs, one subject DP (Meena) and TWO predicate DPs. (her spouse) and (a surprise gift). The verb *give* needs a minimum of three DPs to accomplish its course of action.

Sentence 4 comprises one subject DP (Asok), one predicate DP the bouquet) and a PP. (on his table) here, the verb place needs two DPs and a PP to complete its composition.

In traditional usage, verbs are classified into three categories: transitive, intransitive, and ditransitive. It specifies the number of objects a verb can engage in the VP. An intransitive verb is defined by its inability to accommodate objects. When a verb takes one object, it is known as transitive. If a verb takes two objects, a direct object and an indirect object, it is known as a ditransitive verb. In traditional grammar, DPs in the VP are only the arguments of the verb, while in generative grammar, subject DPs are also arguments of the verb. It means that the verb ultimately decides the roles of all nouns in a sentence. The argument structure refers to how a verb determines the role of nouns in a sentence. It is possible to incorporate this idea differently, specifying the minimum number of participating elements required for the predicate to express the action or state. The semantic issues of the sentence are partially addressed in such a way that the linguistic aspects of each word are matched to the formation of the sentence. We can learn more about how the verb assigns roles to each argument in the theta theory.

THETA THEORY

To move forward with Theta theory, we must clarify how we categorise verbs according to Chomsky's legacy and the traditional approach. As previously stated, verbs in traditional English are subcategorised based on their ability to engage with one or multiple objects. Regarding subcategorising generative grammar, the distribution of DPs and PPs is crucial. A word's distributional properties help us understand where and why it is in a particular location in a sentence.

*Boy, the walks five kilometres daily.

The sentence's ungrammaticality is due to the incorrect distribution of the determiner.

The following distribution represents a sentence's minimum appearance of DPs and PPs.

1. DP VP (V) Raju slept.
2. DP VP (V-DP) Moisen met his friend.
3. DP VP (V-DP-DP). The Swamy gave his followers a gift.
4. DP-VP-(V-DP-PP). The boy placed the toy in his cupboard.

The word's distributional property tells us where it occurs in a sentence. As we discussed earlier in the argument structure, it is essential to remember that the word is present for a reason.

Some issues are raised here, such as the relations between the DPs (the arguments of the verbs) in the sentence and what promotes or decides these specific relations. Theta theory can address any issues related to this, as well as many related to semantic issues.

THEMATIC ROLE (THETA ROLE)

The theta role is a term used by verbs to describe the relationship between the verb's arguments or predicate in a particular sentence. Theta role, which is elaborately called thematic role, explicitly shows us how the arguments are related. However, the problem here is that although it is essential, it is tough to distinguish between them as narrow lines divide them. So, thematic differences are not universally agreed upon by writers.

1. The old man slept.

   In the sentence, the verb slept is a one-place predicate, so it only needs one argument, namely the subject DP, to accomplish its duty. The DP, 'the old man', performs the act of sleeping, and the verb assigns the thematic role of AGENT.

2. The boy hit the girl.

   In the second sentence, the verb 'hit' must have two arguments to complete its course of action: in other words, it's a two-place argument verb. The first argument is that the boy is hitting, and the girl is being hit or affected by it. Hence, one who hits is an AGENT, and the other is a PATIENT.

3. The child noticed the bird.

   In the third sentence, the verb 'noticed' is also a two-place verb that requires two arguments, and the child and the bird are the two. Here, the child is the one who notices and hence is performing as the AGENT. But the bird is not affected by the act of noticing, so its thematic role is not PATIENT but THEME.

4. John likes gardening.

   In sentence 4, the verb like is a two-place verb that requires a minimum of two arguments, but the subject, John, is not a performer for the verb like. John is experiencing gardening, and because of this, he is not an AGENT but an EXPERIENCER. And, of course, John experiences gardening, and its thematic role is THEME.

5. Joseph rushed towards the hospital.

   In sentence 5, Joseph is 'rushing', which means that he is the AGENT, and the action is an ongoing process towards a destination. So, the thematic role of 'hospital' is GOAL.

6. Sali bought her cosmetics from a supermarket.

   In sentence 6, the verb 'bought' is a two-place argument. The doer of 'bringing' is Sali (AGENT), and what she bought is her cosmetics (THEME). There is another argument in the sentence 'a supermarket (SOURCE), from where Sali bought.

7. The principal issued the certificate to the participant.

   In sentence 7, the verb issued is a three-argument verb that assigns the roles of AGENT and THEME to the NPs, the principal and THEME, respectively. However, the theta assigned to 'the participants' is BENIFICIARY or GOAL.

8. The statue entertained the visitors.

   In Sentence 8, the verb 'entertained' is a two-place verb, meaning it can have two arguments. Unlike the examples above, the subject argument is inanimate, so the theta role assigned to it is not AGENT but THEME.

9. The minister was in Delhi.

   In sentence 9, the minister is the subject DP, who happened to be in a place without any deliberate effort. So, the theta role is not AGENT but THEME, and in Delhi, it is a PP, which is LOCATION.

The summarisation of the theta roles will consist of the following.

1. AGENT: the deliberate actor/doer who initiates an action from which it acquires the 'theta' role.
2. PATIENT: the person or thing to whom an action has an effect directly or indirectly.
3. THEME: the person or thing that is moved or becomes stationary or a topic by action.
4. LOCATION: the place that marks the position of something the verb expresses.
5. EXPERIENCER: an animate being that experiences certain emotions, states of being, or a perception expressed by the verb.
6. BENIFICIARY: the person or thing that benefits from the action expressed by the verb.
7. SOURCE: the entity from which something happens to move because of the action expressed by the verb.
8. GOAL: the entity towards which the verb's action moves something.

THETA GRID

Theta grid is the way that thematic properties are represented in the lexicon. It is essential to understand that the theta roles and thematic relations differ. Although a DP may have multiple thematic relationships, it has only one thematic role assigned to it.

1. Raju gave some money to his grandmother.

    The DP Raju has two thematic relations in the sentence: AGENT and SOURCE. As Raju is an actor, performing the act of giving is an AGENT, while money is going from Raju and hence a SOURCE. But the verb assigns Raju the theta role as the only AGENT. This information for a verb in the lexicon is essential and represented as a table called theta grid.

AGENT DP
i

1. Smile(v)

    The theta grid table indicates that the word smile is a one-place verb with a subject DP as the only argument, and it is indexed as 'i' in the second row.

    EX. The boy smiled.

AGENT DP	PATIENT GOAL DP
i	j

2. Hit (v)

The two columns of the table indicate that the verb 'hit' requires a minimum of two arguments to complete its course of action. The first column says the verb 'hit' has a subject DP (the underlining denotes the subject), and the theta role is AGENT. The second row shows that it is indexed by 'i'. In the second column, the first row indicates that the verb has an interior DP that is a PATIENT or THEME by its theta role. The second row in the second column indicates that the DP is indexed with the letter 'j'.

EX: the boy hit the girl.

EXPERIENCER DP	PP
i	j

3. Believe (v)

The Theta grid of the verb 'believe' states that it is a two-place verb that requires an EXPERIENCER as the subject and a PP argument as the predicate. The two arguments are indexed as 'i' and 'j'.

Ex: The man believed in God.

4. Give (V)

AGENT SOURCE DP	GOAL BENEFICIARY DP	THEME GOAL DP/PP
i	j	k

The table shows that the verb needs a minimum of three arguments to accomplish its task. However, AGENT or SOURCE is the thematic relations of the subject DP; the one assigned as AGENT, which is indexed as i, is the only one that has the theta role assigned to them. The second column says that the first interior DP may be GOAL or BENEFICIARY depending on its distribution, and it is indexed as *j*. The third column states that the second interior argument can be either DP or PP depending on the distribution chosen, and it is indexed as '*k*'.

Ex: 1. John gave the beggar some money.

2. John gave some money to the beggar.

AGENT	THEME	PP
i	j	k

5. Place(v)

According to the theta grid table of 'place', it is a 3-place verb, requiring a minimum of three arguments to complete its course of action. There is a subject DP assigned as an AGENT, a predicate DP assigned as THEME, and a PP in which there is a DP assigned as the LOCATION.

Ex: Babu placed the book in his bag.

THETA CRITERIA

1. Each argument is assigned one and only one theta role.
2. Each theta role is assigned to one and only one argument.

Certain elements, such as expletives and adjuncts, are not assigned a theta role in a sentence. Expletives are words like 'it', 'there', etc., which are probably used at the beginning of a sentence only to avoid the compulsory filling up of the empty slot in the subject DP.

Ex: it is raining. ('it' in the sentence is an expletive.)

On the other hand, adjuncts are optional entities without which the sentence is complete.

Ex: The boy slept on a mattress. In this sentence, the PP 'on the mattress' is an optional adjunct, so no theta role will be assigned to it.

Apart from these exceptions, any omission or inclusion of words in a sentence will result in ungrammaticality.

1. *The girl smiled the friend $_J$

   Smile: (v)

AGENT DP	?
i	j

In sentence 1, the verb smile is a single-argument verb. However, there is an additional argument, 'the friend,' which is indexed by 'j', but no theta role is assigned, so the sentence becomes ungrammatical.

2. *The desk smiled.

   Smile:(v)

AGENT DP
i

In sentence 2, as the theta grid table shows, there is only one argument for the verb 'smile'. However, the argument is not qualified to be an AGENT subject because it is not an initiator or doer.

3. The girl smiled at her parents.

   Sentence 3 is grammatical even though it has an optional PP argument, as the PP in the sentence is optional and does not require the theta role.

4. *The magician$_i$ opened.

   Open: (v)

AGENT DP	THEME
I	j

   Sentence 4 becomes ungrammatical because the THEME is absent.

5. The magician $_i$ opened to the audience $_j$.

   In sentence 5, another argument is indexed as j, but it's a PP instead of a THEME, which makes it ungrammatical.

6. The magician $_i$ opened the box $_j$.

   Sentence 6 is acceptable as it adheres to the theta criteria.

7. *The collector allotted.
8. * The collector allotted teachers.
9. * The collector allotted election duties.
10. *The collector allotted to the teachers.
11. The collector allotted the teachers election duties.

12. The collector allotted election duties to the teachers.

Let's examine why sentences 7, 8, 9, and 10 are grammatically unacceptable.

AGENT DP	THEME/GOAL DP/PP	GOAL/THEME PP/DP
i	j	k

Allot (v)

The verb 'allot' is a three-place argument indexed by 'i', 'j', and 'k' and sets the theta roles as AGENT, 'THEME/GOAL' and 'GOAL/THEME'. Without these roles and proper indices, the sentence is incomplete and ungrammatical.

The theta criteria must be met for sentences in all other verb categories on the theta grid to be grammatical. To put it briefly, thematic relations reveal the true nature of arguments and the semantic appropriateness of the words in a sentence. Furthermore, they behave accordingly by the assigned theta role by the predicate, and the theta grid helps us understand how the words fit in a sentence. When we say a verb requires certain types of arguments, we mean that the verb can select that argument category to accomplish its purpose. The technical term we give to this phenomenon is categorical selection or c-selection. If the selection depends on semantic obligations, we call it s-selection. The other term that we use to describe the concept is subcategorisation. When a verb only requires one DP to compete with the sentence, we can also say that the verb is subcategorised for a single DP.

CLAUSAL ARGUMENTS

We have already discussed the obligatory arguments required for a predicate or subject to create an acceptable grammatical sentence. When a sentence replaces such an obligatory DP or PP, we call it a clausal argument. In other words, when a clause serves as an argument, it is called a clausal argument.

For example.

1. The headmistress announced the holidays.
2. The headmistress announced that the next three days would be holidays.

From the examples above, it can be inferred that the verb 'announce' is a two-place verb capable of complementing either a DP or a clause. So, the verb's theta grid could be as follows,

Announce, (v)

DP	DP/S
i	J

A. Gita surprised all her classmates.
B. That Gita secured a first-class surprised all her classmates.

Examples A and B show that Gita, a DP in A, is replaced by a clause introduced by that. As a result, the verb is labelled in its theta grid as follows.

Surprise: (v)

DP/S	DP
i	J

1. That Gita secured a first-class surprise all her classmates.
2. It surprised all her classmates that Gita secured a first-class.

Both sentences 1 and 2 express the same as paraphrases. However, in sentence 2, 'it' has no theta role even though it sits in the subject place. As we discussed earlier, the word 'It' in the sentence is not a pronoun but rather an expletive with no theta role.

The clausal argument, as in the context discussed above, can be either a finite clause or an infinitival one.

For example,

1. They preferred the girls' entrance to the hall first.
2. They preferred that the girls enter the hall first.
3. They preferred for the girls to enter the hall first.
4. They preferred the girls to enter the hall first.

In sentence 1, the complement of the verb is a DP, but in sentence 2, it is a clausal argument of a finite clause. Whereas in sentences 3 and 4, they are infinitive clauses.

PREDICATE ADJECTIVES

Our discussion so far has focused on how various verbs assign arguments thematic roles. However, arguments are assigned their theta role by adjectives when they are the predicate of a sentence.

1. The boy is tall.

   In the above example, the adjective 'tall' is the predicate and a one-place adjective. The labelling for its theta grid is as follows:

Tall: (adjective)

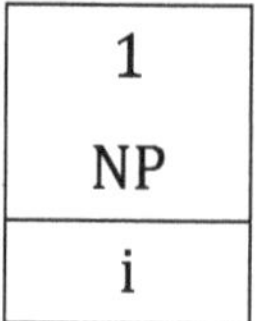

1 NP
i

2. The boy is fond of pets.

   In the second example, the adjective 'fond' is used as the predicate and is a two-place adjective. Therefore, its theta grid is labelled as follows:

1 NP	2 PP
i	j

PREDICATE PREPOSITION

As in the case of adjectives discussed above, prepositions are also in the predicate position, which will determine the theta role.

1. The president is in Delhi.

   In example 1, the preposition 'in' is the predicate, and to determine its theta role, it is considered a one-place preposition. Therefore, its theta grid is labelled as follows:

   In: (preposition)

1 NP
i

2. The village is between the river and the hills.

   Since the preposition 'between' is a three-place preposition, its theta role is labelled as follows.

   Between: (preposition)

1 NP	2 NP	3 NP
i	J	k

Before moving on to other topics, we must discuss two important matters related to the ones we have been discussing so far.

PROJECTION PRINCIPLES

Based on the discussions above, we understand that lexical items, as the heads of phrases, construct the constituents to create all kinds of clauses and sentences. Their selection is determined by their ability to perform syntactical and semantic tasks. In addition, they could assign the theta role to entries. The minimum requirements encoded in the theta grid almost determine the entire structure of the sentence. Thus, each component is assigned a theta role regardless of whether they are there due to C-Selection (Categorical selection) or S-Selection (Semantical selection).

This is called Projection Principles.

EXTENDED PROJECTION PRINCIPLES.

As per the projection principles, all lexical entries are assigned their theta role, but there are certain words without a theta role, like expletives. The reason for the presence of these words is that English is not a pro-drop language. The pro-drop languages can drop the subject because, without the subject, all the relationships are evident in those languages. In other words, the subject place should not be empty in English. So, the place should be filled with alternatives, like expletives, even though they are not assigned the theta role. This is a language-specific requirement for non-pro drop languages like English, known as the Extended Projection Principle.

CASE THEORY

So far, we have discussed thematic relationships in detail, but now it is time to examine the details of structural relationships. We will discuss case theory in this regard and then move on to other topics. Case theory, in its simplest form, explains that each DP, regardless of their position, is assigned a case. In a primary sense, the subject and object DPs are assigned the nominal case and accusative case, respectively.

When comparing proper and common nouns with pronouns, the cases can easily be seen morphologically in the pronouns. However, whether morphologically seen or not, all DPs are assigned to cases. When nouns or pronouns are not morphologically overt, like 'it', 'Babu', or 'you' in all cases, they are in the abstract case. Having established this, let us examine the morphological differences between pronouns, proper nouns, and common nouns as they help observe.

I, we, you, he, she, they, it, John, Mary

Nominative	Accusative	Genitive	Dative
I	me	my	me
we	us	our	us
you	you	your	you
he	him	his	him

she	her	her	her
they	them	their	them
it	it	its	it
John	John	John's	John
Mary	Mary	Mary's	Mary
the man	the man	the man's	the man

1. I love her.
2. She loves me.

In the first and second sentences, 'her' and 'she' refer to the third person singular, but in the first sentence, it is 'her' and 'she' in the second. This is because they are both associated with and assigned to different categories of cases. In the first sentence, 'her' is the object, and in the second sentence, 'she' is the subject. Therefore, they are assigned to different cases.

At this point, we can also observe that cases are assigned not to the entity but instead depending on their distribution, like the thematic roles. To put it another way, when 'she' moves from the subject to the object place, the case, too, changes. A case is defined as a grammatical category that can be based on either semantic or syntactic function.

We have discussed the thematic relationship and concluded that each noun is assigned a theta-role by the inert qualities of verbs, especially categorisation. Similarly, all nouns and pronouns will have cases according to their positions, which means that the theory of cases restricts a sentence's ungrammaticality. This mechanism is known as a case filter as it restricts the construction of sentences without proper case assignments, either abstract or morphological, to an overt noun.

1. She has attacked him.

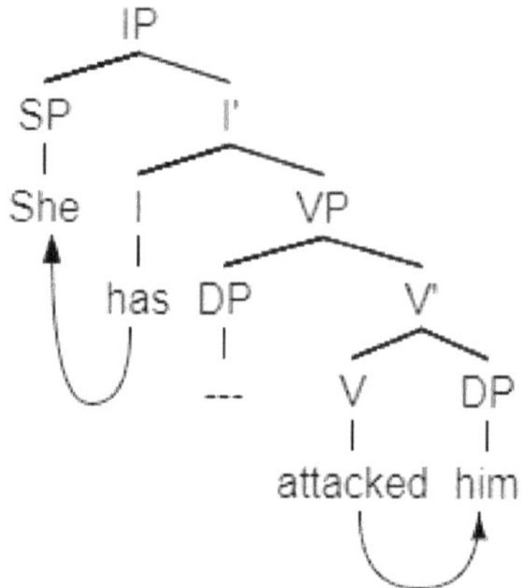

In the above sentence, she is in the subject position and 'him' is in the object position, and the diagram shows how they got the case assignment. As per the diagram representation, the inflexion 'has', notated by 'I', assigns the nominative case to 'she', while the verb 'attacked' assigns the accusative case to 'him'.

2. John's mother will give a gift to him.

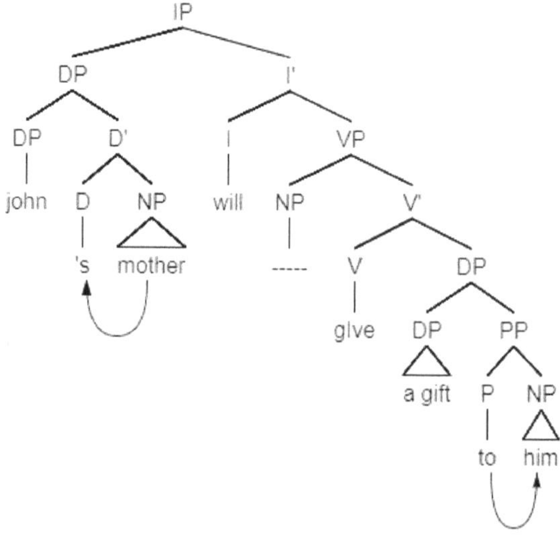

The diagram of sentence 2 shows that the genitive case (John's) case assigner is the NP, while that of the dative case is the preposition (to him).

What basis do they assign the case? That's the next question. To fully appreciate it, we must understand government and binding theory.

Let us recall specific terms that we mentioned earlier informally.

Dominance: Node A dominates node B if and only if A is a higher node than B in a tree and can trace a line from A to B downwards.

3.

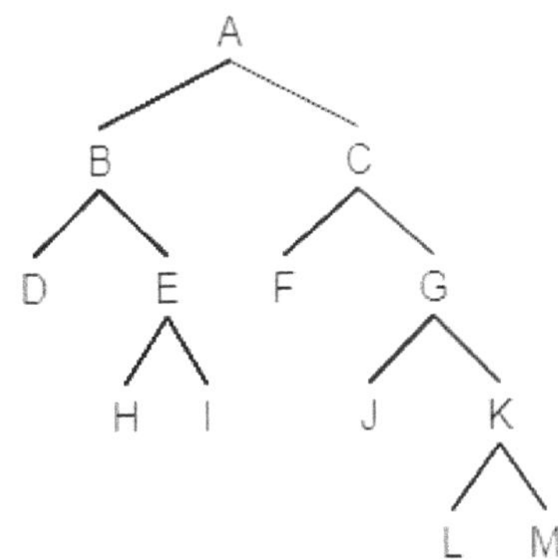

In the above example, A dominates all other nodes, while B only dominates D, E, H, and I. C dominates F, G, J, K, L, and M, not any other nodes. G only dominates J, K, L, and M, and K dominates L and M. E dominates only H and I.

C-Command: (i). A c-command B if and if only A does not dominate B or B does not dominate A.

(ii). The first branching node that dominates A also dominates B.

(iii). If A c-commands B, it also c-commands all other nodes that B dominate.

a. In diagram 3, B c-command C and all other nodes that C dominate (F, G, J, K, L and M).

b. F c-command G and all other nodes that G dominates (J, K, L and M).

c. J c-command K and all other nodes K dominates (L&M).

d. L c-command M.

e. C c-command B and all other nodes that B dominates (D, E, H & I).

f. I c-command H.

We can also observe that the c-command relationship is mainly between sister nodes, and sister nodes c-command each other. When two nodes c-command each other, it is called Symmetric c-command, otherwise called asymmetric c-command. For example, in our given diagram, B c-commands G, but G does not c-command B. This is an asymmetric c-command.

Government: A governs B if and only if

i. A c-command B and B c-command A

ii. A is a governor.

iii. The governor is the head

4.

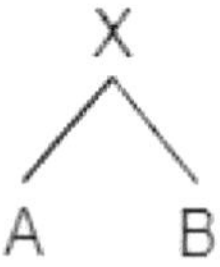

In the diagram above, A c-commands B and B c-commands A, and the first branching node X dominates A and B, and A is the head. Therefore, we will say that A governs B.

M-command: The notion mentioned above by the government had to be modified later on specific empirical grounds and the evidence available in the literature. As per the later version,

A governs B if and only if

i. A is a governor,

ii. A m-commands B, and

iii. No barriers between A and B

Here, a Maximal projection is mentioned as a barrier.

5.

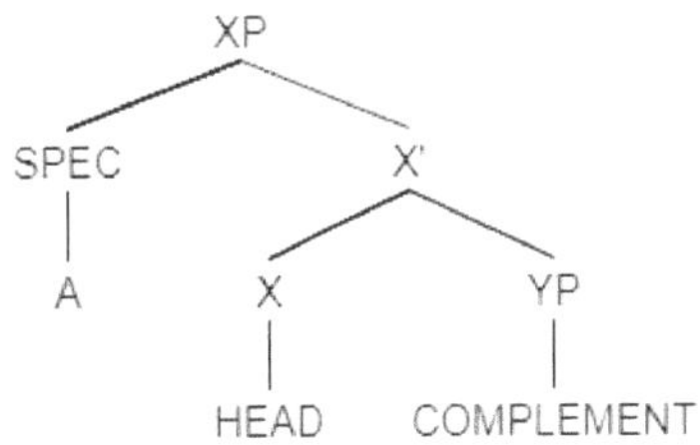

Diagram 5 shows the difference between the c-command and the m-command. As per the c-command, according to the diagram, HEAD c-commands COMPLEMENT as they are sisters, and the first branching node X' dominates both nodes, so there are no barriers to intervention. Whereas m-command is concerned, X' is not counted as a barrier so that the HEAD m-commands both specifier and complement. Maximal projection (XP) is considered as the branching node that dominates A and B, and so the government principle is modified as

A governs B if and only if

i. A is a governor,

ii. A m-commands B and

iii. There is no maximal projection between A and B

iv. Governors are heads.

Precedence: Node A precedes B if and only if A falls left of B and A and B do not dominate each other.

Antecedent: An NP that gives meaning and reference to an anaphor or a pronoun is known as an antecedent. An antecedent does not need to precede the anaphor or pronoun to which it gives meaning.

BINDING THEORY

We come across different types of NPs, which can be broadly classified into three:

a. **R-expressions**: They are standard or proper nouns that acquire meaning from the world; to say, they refer to some entity in the world. (Ex, Shanker, Rose, tree, woman, etc.)
b. **Pronouns:** They may gain meaning from the sentence in which they occur or from the context of the world. (he, she, they, etc.) and
c. **Anaphors:** Anaphors receive their meaning from an entity in the sentence, to say they refer back to something or someone (antecedent) in the sentence in which they occur. (Ex, himself, herself, herself, ourselves, each other, etc.).

The binding theory explicitly defines the connections between all of them.

A binds B if and only if

i. A c-commands B and
ii. A and B are co-indexed.

Binding principles A, B, and C:

A. An Anaphor must be bound within its binding domain.

B. A pronoun must be accessible in its binding domain.

C. An R-expression must be free everywhere.

Let us examine this by observing a few examples.

6. John hit himself.

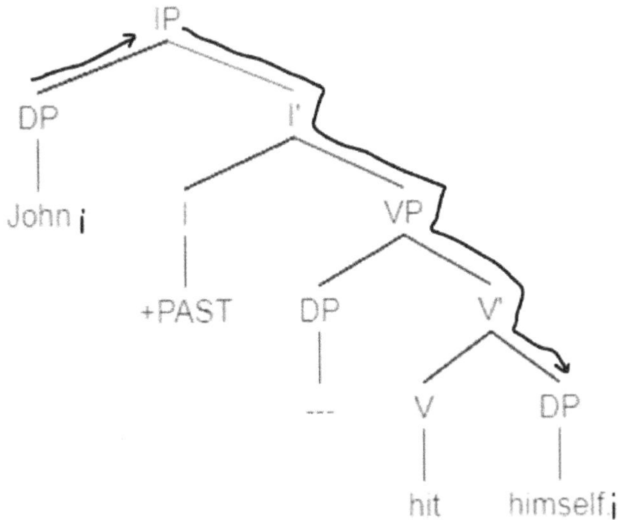

i. The NP 'John' and the anaphor 'himself' are co-indexed with 'i'.

ii. John c-commands himself

iii. And both 'John' and himself are in the same domain.

As all the conditions of binding principle A are met, the sentence is acceptable.

7. Mary said that herself danced with John.

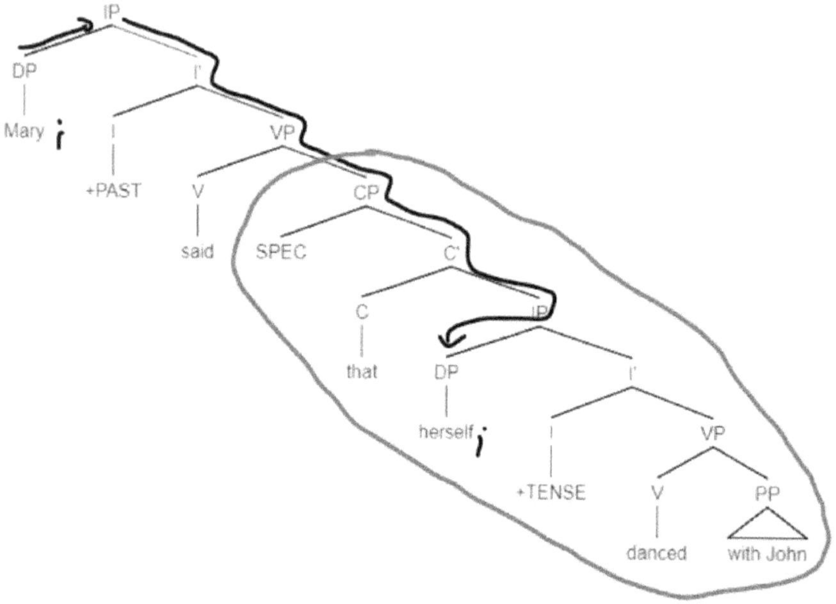

i. DP Mary is co-indexed with DP 'herself'.

ii. Mary c-commands 'herself', but 'herself' is part of another CP and falls within a different domain. The sentence is ungrammatical because it violates the binding rule A.

8. Sita liked her.

We can interpret the pronoun 'her' in two ways. In one way, it can be co-indexed with Sita, but in another way, they are both indexed differently. When they are co-indexed, the sentence is ungrammatical as it violates the binding principle B. But the sentence becomes all right when it is indexed with two indices.

9. Sita said that she liked ice cream.

Sentence 9 is acceptable, though 'Sita' and 'she' are co-indexed and bound; they belong to different binding domains. The sentence is also grammatical even when the two entities are indexed with two indices, as the pronoun 'she' is free then.

10. a) $John_k$ hit him_k.

b) $john_k$ hit him_l

In the above examples, in sentence a, 'John' and 'him' are co-indexed with k, but in the following sentence, John is indexed with 'k' and him is indexed with 'l'. John is an R-expression, and it must be free everywhere. However, when it is co-indexed and bound in a sentence, it becomes ungrammatical. Whereas in sentence b, John is indexed with 'k', and 'him' is indexed with 'l', so they are not co-referential, and the sentence is all right.

PRO

We have talked about embedded clauses multiple times before, and we will continue doing so in the future with different aspects in mind. There are two types of clauses: finite and non-finite, which are also called infinitive clauses. In the first type of clause, there is a tensed verb, but in the second type, there is an infinitive verb. The more important thing about the non-finite clause is that its subject is always non-overt but takes interpretation from a DP in the sentence. The non-overt pronominal DP exists in the D-structure with all the theta roles and case marks. Such a non-overt DP of an infinitive clause is the PRO. This is also known as Big PRO as it has a competitor written as '*pro*', which is also an empty category of pronoun in a pro-drop language.

We can analyse this using a diagram of a sentence with a non-finite clause.

1. I decided to go to the seawall.

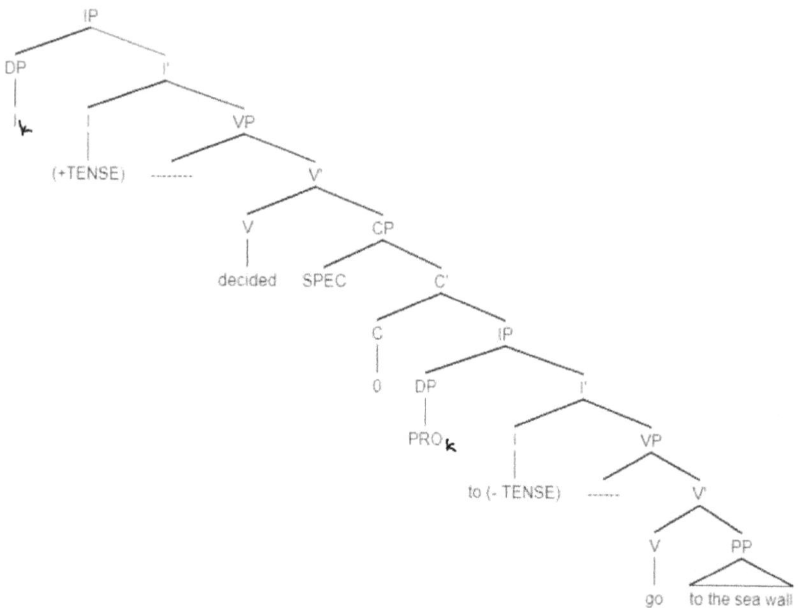

The diagram shows that the verb 'to go' in the subordinate clause has a non-overt subject (PRO), which is co-indexed with the subject of the main clause 'I'. The co-indexing indicates that the main clause subject interprets the PRO. If the non-overt pronoun (PRO) had been pronounced, it would have been read as 'I decided (I)to go to the seawall'.

The Extended Projection Principle requires a subject for every clause, whether it is finite or infinitive. So, it becomes mandatory to have a subject. As syntactical representation is compulsory, it is necessary to use a PRO element in place of the subject.

It is also important to note that a DP controls the PRO as it interprets it. The DP that controls the PRO can also be called a controller.

2. a) $Mary_k$ promised $Thomas_l$ PRO_k to complete the work.

   b) $Mary_m$ persuaded $Thomas_n$ PRO_n to complete the work.

The construction of 2(a) and 2(b) appears to be identical. But in 2(a), the agent of the verb 'promised' and 'to complete' are the same, and they are co-indexed with 'k'. It means that Mary, not Thomas, controls PRO. Meanwhile, in sentence 2(b), Mary is the agent of the verb 'promise', but Thomas is the agent of the verb 'complete'; therefore, they are co-indexed. In the first sentence, Mary is the subject of the sentence, and in the second sentence, Thomas is the object of the verb 'persuaded'. So, we say the first one is called subject-controlled PRO, and the second one is an example of object-controlled PRO.

CONTROL VERB AND RAISING VERB

3 (a) Raju appeared to fix the computer.

  (b) Raju wanted to fix the computer.

The two sentences are identical in construction, but a closer look reveals that they are very different due to the lexical properties of the verbs. The verb 'appeared' is a one-place verb to which an agent argument may not be possible, as voluntary 'appearing' is impossible. 'Appeared' is not done by Raju, but 'fixing' is done. Therefore, Raju is the initiator or agent of 'fixing'. In the second sentence, the verb 'wanted' is a two-place verb and has an agent as its subject. If we analyse the sentences using tree diagrams, the picture will be more precise.

3 (a) Raju appeared to fix the computer.

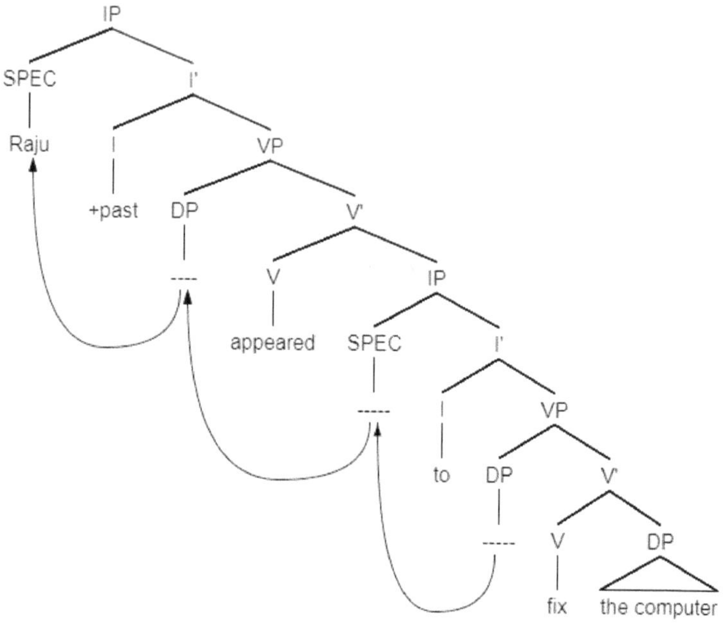

The diagram clearly shows that Raju is the subject of the verb 'fix'. But it cannot get its case from 'to', so it moves to a higher node until the Spec node gets a nominative case. Moreover, it is not in an argumentative position where it originated to make the movement mandatory. However, the sentence in 3 (b) is different.

(b) Raju wanted to fix the computer.

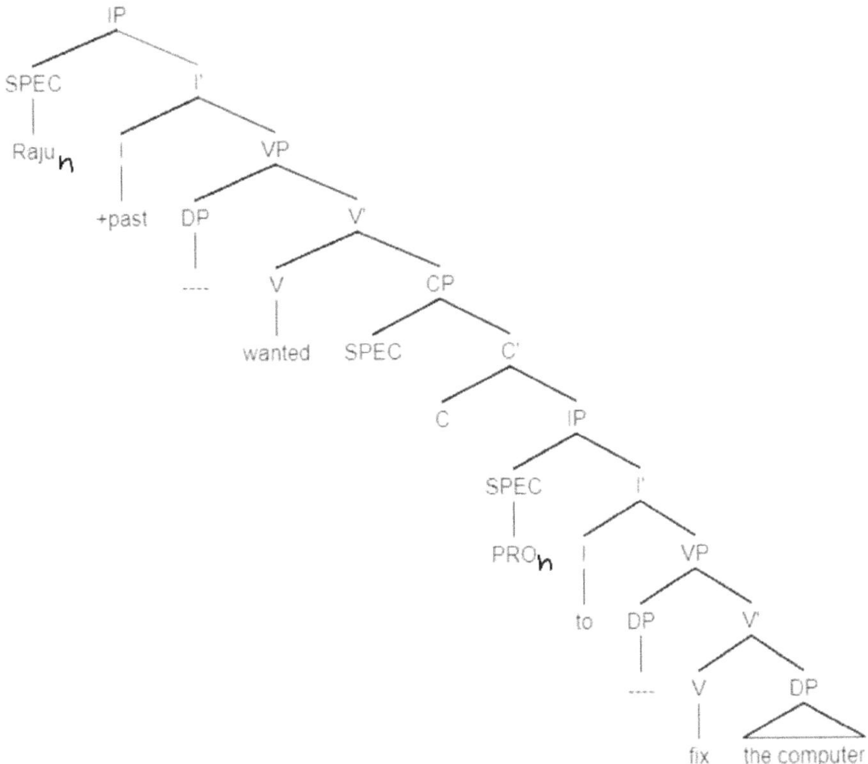

The diagram displays that the verb 'to fix' lacks a subject, which is obligatory for an argumentative position. So, the non-overt DP PRO was inserted and co-indexed.

3 (a) is an example of a raising verb, but 3(b) is an example of controlling verb.

Synopsis of the Chapter

The Principles and Parameters (P&P) Theory, proposed by Noam Chomsky, is a cornerstone of Generative Grammar that explains how universal principles and language-specific parameters interact to generate grammatically correct sentences across all human languages.

This theory reduces the complexity of learning a language by assuming that universal principles are innate while parameters are set through exposure to a specific language. It provides a framework for analysing syntactic phenomena such as argument structure, thematic roles, projection principles, case theory, and binding theory.

1. Principles and Parameters

- Principles: Universal rules that apply to all languages, ensuring a common syntactic foundation.
- Example: The Theta Criterion (discussed below) applies universally.
- Parameters: Language-specific settings that account for variation.
- Example: The head-directionality parameter determines whether a language is head-initial (e.g., English) or head-final (e.g., Japanese).

2. Argument Structure and Theta Theory

- Arguments of Verbs: Verbs and predicates require a specific number and type of arguments (subjects, objects, etc.) to form grammatical sentences.
- Theta Theory: Describes the assignment of thematic roles (theta roles) to the arguments of predicates.
- Thematic Roles: Agent, Theme, Experiencer, Goal, etc.
- Theta Grid: A representation of the thematic roles associated with a predicate.
- Example: "Give" requires three arguments: Agent (giver), Theme (item), and Goal (recipient).
- Theta Criterion: Ensures that each argument is assigned one and only one theta role, and every theta role must be assigned.

3. Projection Principles

Projection Principle: The syntactic structure of a sentence must represent all lexical properties of its elements, including argument structure.

Extended Projection Principle (EPP): Every sentence must have a subject, even if it is implied (e.g., "It is raining").

4. Case Theory

- Ensures that all noun phrases (NPs) in a sentence are assigned case:
- Nominative Case: Assigned to subjects by finite verbs.
- Accusative Case: Assigned to objects by transitive verbs.
- Genitive Case: Assigned to possessors.
- Case Filter: Prevents NPs from appearing in the surface structure without case.

5. Government and Binding

- Government Theory: Describes the hierarchical relationship between elements in a sentence:
- Dominance: A node dominates another if it is higher in the tree.
- C-command: A node c-commands another if it governs it and does not dominate it.
- Government: A node governs another if it assigns a case or links syntactic elements.
- Binding Theory: Explains the relationships between pronouns, anaphors, and their antecedents:
- Binding Principle A: Anaphors (e.g., "himself") must be bound in their governing domain.

- Binding Principle B: Pronouns (e.g., "he") must not be bound in their governing domain.
- Binding Principle C: R-expressions (e.g., "John") must be free (not bound).

6. PRO, Control Verbs, and Raising Verbs

- PRO: A null pronoun that appears in non-finite clauses and satisfies the Theta Criterion for clauses without subjects.
- Example: "John wants [PRO to leave]."
- Control Verbs: Verbs that determine the referent of PRO.
- Example: "John tried [PRO to swim]" (John = PRO).
- Raising Verbs: Verbs that do not assign a theta role to the subject, causing it to move from an embedded clause.
- Example: "John seems [to be happy]."

7. Clausal Arguments and Predicates

- Clausal Arguments: Clauses can serve as arguments of verbs, often introduced by complementisers (e.g., "that" or "whether").
- Example: "John believes [that Mary is smart.]"
- Predicate Adjectives: Adjectives that describe the subject or object of the clause.
- Example: "John is [happy]."
- Predicate Prepositions: Prepositional phrases functioning as predicates.
- Example: "The book is [on the table]."

8. Binding Theory

- R-Expressions: Referential expressions (e.g., names) must be free.
- Pronouns: Must not have an antecedent within their governing category.
- Anaphors: Must have an antecedent within their governing category.

Our discussion in this chapter focused on the Principles and Parameters (P&P) theory and the Government and Binding theory. This leads us to understand that the first one is the abstract model that distinguishes the universal and language-specific nature of languages. Government and Binding (GB) theory focuses on the relationships between constituents in a sentence's thematic and structural aspects. These two are the foundation for the future advancements of Generative Grammar as the Minimalist Programme. The first one strengthens the universality of grammar suitable for all languages, whereas the second one makes the modularity of sentence construction the key point of minimalism.

CHAPTER VI

MOVEMENTS

We discussed some aspects of movements in one of the previous chapters while discussing Transformational Generative Grammar (TGG). Later, we moved ahead to the X-Bar theory, which is more potent than the earlier versions and could resolve many of the unresolved issues with TGG and PSG. The time has come to discuss movements and other notations from a new perspective, as we now have many different theories and frameworks besides the X-Bar theory. The formation of a new thesis requires the accumulation of new evidence due to fresh hypotheses, which are the constraints of a theory. The phenomenon occurs in all scientific studies, including linguistics, so we move from theory to theory to achieve more perfection.

While discussing Transformational Generative Grammar (TGG), we noticed that words were moving from one place to another, but we called it transformation rather than movement. The reason for this is that each movement took place under different rules, but now we refer to them as movements because they move under the same set of rules. Whether or not movements take place in passivation, relativisation, question formation, topicalisation, or whatever, the motive behind them will be the same. Hence, the same set of rules is applied. The term ' move α' (move alfa) was introduced in this context, implying that anything can move anywhere.

When we start talking about movement, two questions arise: why it takes place and what triggers it. It's important to note that the D-structure of the sentence is where the movements, motives, and all related matters occur, not the S-structure. So, we depend more on expanded D-structure based on X-Bar theory to understand them.

Let's start with the movements that take place within an IP.

1. I met him in the park.

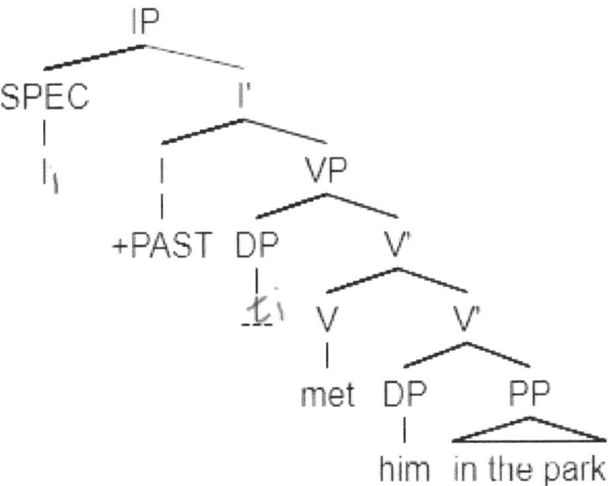

In the above D-structure representation, DP 'I' under VP moves upward to the specifier node. Here, we must assume that the subject DP originates at the node marked 't_i' and later moved upwards for a purpose. Despite moving, the branching node remains marked with its trace as it is retrievable from the D-structure at any time. There could be two motives for the movement. The verb cannot give case and theta roles to the subject DP. To reach an agreement, the subject must precede the inflection node structurally. Metaphorically speaking, leaving its birthplace benefits the focal point of the sentence, which is the subject. It's important to remember that the S-structure does not contain the item that was moved. This is so because when something moves from one place to another, it leaves a trace, but it is not pronounced.

Q-MOVEMENT

Question formations are mainly divided into two categories: yes/no questions and content questions. Yes/No questions are called, as their expected answers are yes/no. Traditionally, they are called auxiliary questions or auxiliary inversion as they begin with an auxiliary. As a matter of fact, the word inversion may not be an apt one as the return movement of something has not taken place. However, the fronting of the tense, explicitly speaking, and the front movement of the inflection element are the very matters behind question formation. A-Movement and A'-Movement are the two main movements that pertain to all movements. When some items in an argument position are moved, they are called A-movements; otherwise, A'-movements. In all types of movements, constraints that must be met include the theta criterion, +Q +Wh condition, case filters, and the Extended Projection Principle (EPP).

Structure-Preserving Principle

Another constraint that we must be careful about is the preservation of structure. This means that the syntactically established representations in the D-structure should also be intact in the S-structure. This is an additional requirement beyond what we have discussed earlier. Even the position or projection level of specific categories cannot be changed.

An ideal D-structure diagram for an IP, when it is part of a CP, would look like the one given below.

CP
SPEC C'
C IP
DP I'
I NegP
Neg'
Neg AgrP
Agr'
Agr AdvP
Adv'
Adv AspP
Asp'
Asp VP
DP VP'
V XP
Complement

We only highlight essential branches for convenience and compactness, but they're still present. As we have observed, a trace is left behind when anything is moved from one location to another, and it cannot be removed. These trace parts are not pronounced; hence, they do not appear in the S-structure. Let's explore how movements occur when a Y/N question comes up.

2. John has got the letter.

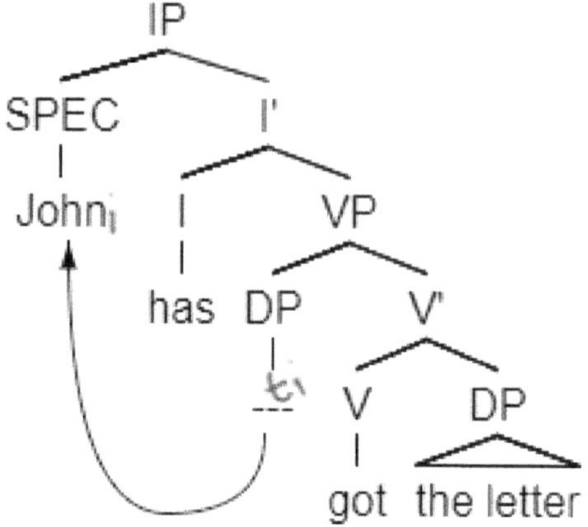

We know that fronting the question particle (in English, an inflectional element) makes this sentence a 'Y/N' question, but there are no more slots available in the IP. So, it must move out of the domain, which means that the IP will become part of a CP.

3. Has John got the letter?

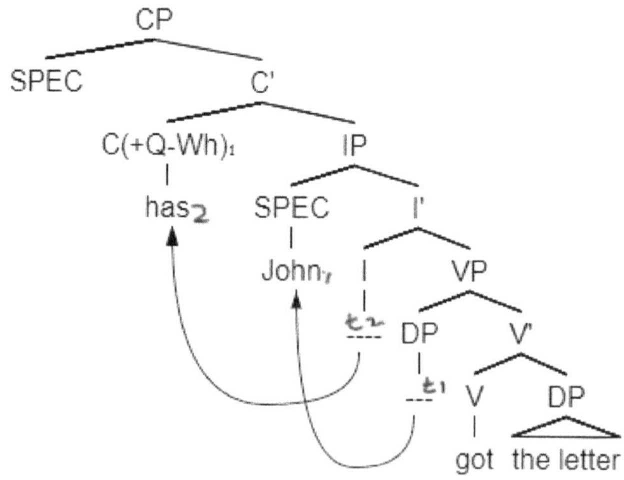

The tree diagram of the question allows us to observe the movements that took place and the traces they left when they moved. To be a question, the inflection element 'has' moves to the COMP position, which is also known as the 'I' to 'C' movement. Significantly, a functional category entity moves to the same category as an argumentative position entity moves to a similar location. This enables them to maintain their theta criterion and case.

Now, let's see what happens when a Y/N question becomes an embedded question.

4. Mary asked if John had got the letter.

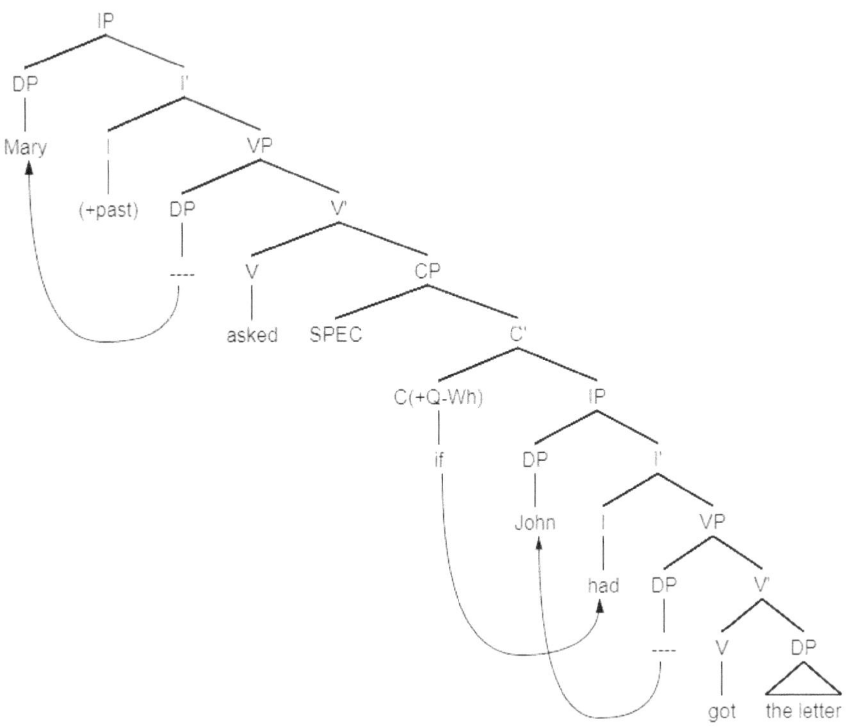

The point to note is that when the question element occurs in the complementiser position, the inflection element returns to the inflection node that was previously a question element.

WH-MOVEMENTS

The movement of question words, generally known as Wh words, to become a content question is called the Wh movement.

1. Who
2. What
3. Which
4. Whose
5. Where
6. When
7. Why
8. How

The Wh-words, including How, although not starting with 'Wh', have different positions in a sentence, and their movement falls under both categories. 1, 2, 3, and 4, along with their complex varieties, belong to DP positions or argument positions, while 6, 7, and 8 belong to adjunct positions. And 'Where' takes both positions. To put it succinctly, both A-movements and A' movements are present in wh-movements. However, irrespective of the position they moved from, they land in the same place, the Spec position of the CP. This is a departure from the movements we have observed so far. In other movements, we witnessed that a phrase in a particular position moved to a similar position mainly due to the maintenance of case filters and the theta criteria. Hence, it's clear that the motivation behind the movement should be seen from a different perspective.

1. Who did you speak to?
2. What do you know?
3. Whose idea do you want to propagate?
4. Which one do you like?
5. Where did that come from?
6. When will you come back?
7. Why do you say Africa instead of the country you mean?
8. How does your sister know it?

To comprehend the motivation behind the Wh-phrase movements, we will examine the D-structure of a few of the sentences mentioned above. As we are aware, it is necessary to adhere to all restrictions, such as the theta criterion, +Q, +/-Wh condition, case filters, and the Extended Projection Principle (EPP).

a. I want to meet the manager.
b. Who do you want to meet?

The position of the manager (the supposed answer) and the WH phrase, which takes a diametrically opposite position, show where it moved from and landed. Now, let's examine the D-structure of the sentence, which may reveal the entire story of the movements.

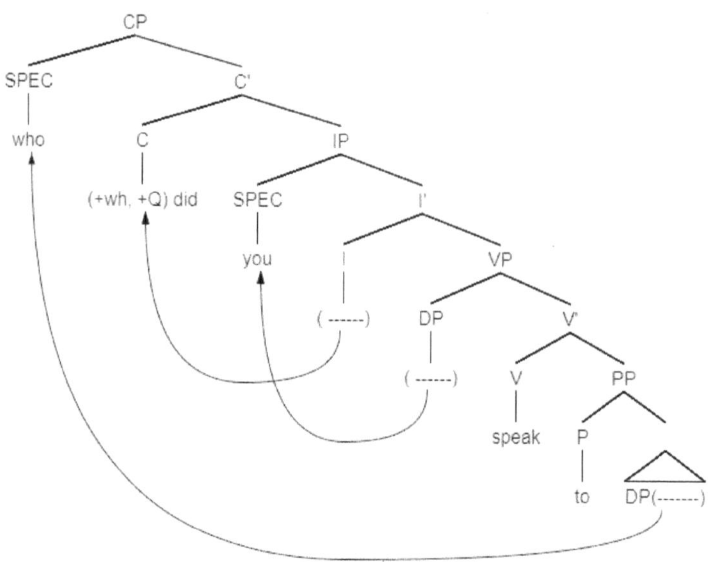

Although 'who' moves from an argumentative position in the DP to the Spec position in the CP, the motivation behind the movement of the phrase is to give the sentence an interpretation of the question. In other words, this movement fulfils the +Wh element. Similarly, the movement of did (auxiliary inversion) satisfies the +Q feature of the sentence. The sentence's legitimacy is enhanced by the theta criterion, case filter, and EPP when the subject 'you' moves from the DP of the VP to the Spec position of the IP.

c. Who did he say wanted bread?

d. Who wants bread?

In our previous example, the object of the preposition was the moving phrase, so the movement was apparent and visible. But when the subject becomes the WH-phrase, movement is not obvious. For example, consider the two sentences. In the first sentence, the subject 'what' moves from its position to the Spec of CP, but in the second sentence, it is unclear if it has been moved at all.

Let's examine the D-structure of sentence 1.

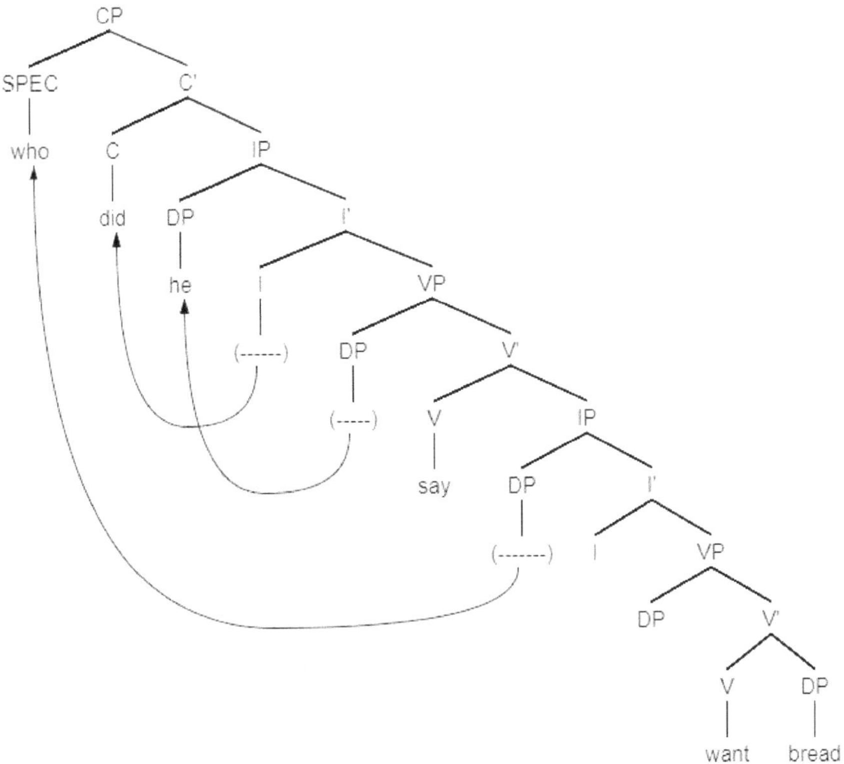

The D-structure diagram illustrates all the movements that enable the sentence to overcome the different kinds of restrictions.

Now see the D structure of sentence 2.

A. He wants bread.

B. Who wants bread?

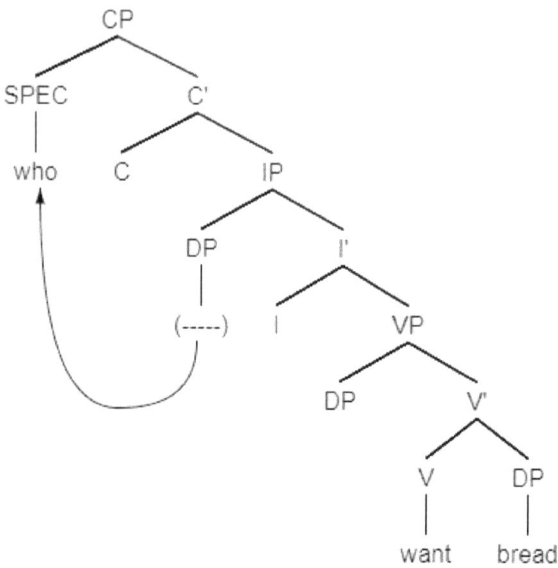

As can be clearly seen, the subject WH-phrase involves movement. The other movements are not shown in the diagram due to their insignificant impact on the D-structure or S-structure. Chomsky referred to this type of movement as **'vacuous'** because it is not apparent in the S-structure.

e. I will come back <u>tomorrow</u>.

f. <u>When</u> will you come back?

In the above example, the moved WH- phrase is an adverbial phrase. In this case, we know that the landing site is the Spec of the CP that we create for question formation. During previous discussion examples, it was observed that movements that start from an argumentative location end up in a non-argumentative site. To conclude, all the Wh movements are A' movements.

g. I said that the principal would come tomorrow.

h. When did you say that the principal would come?

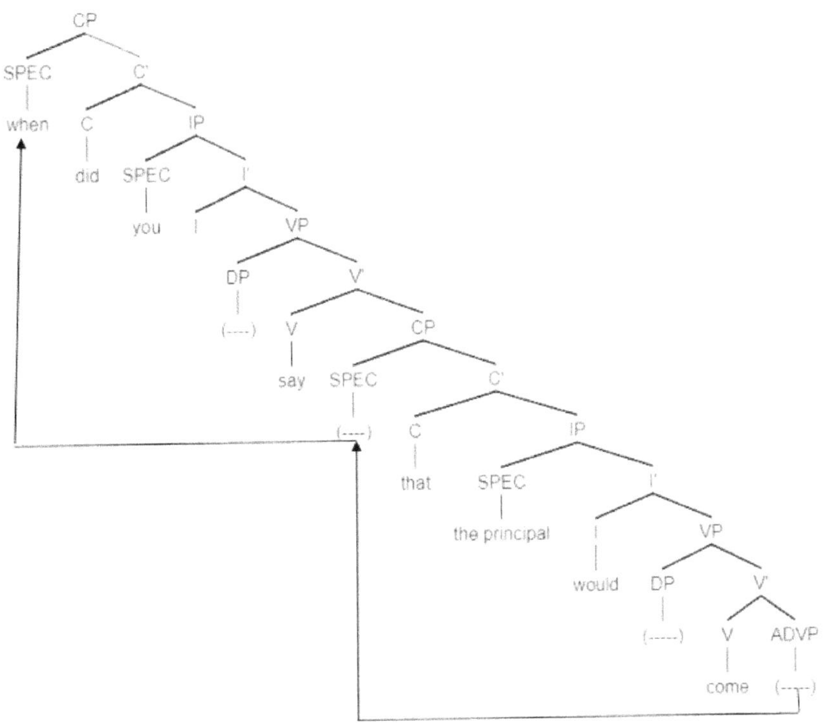

The peculiarity of this movement is that the moving element moves beyond its CP boundary, which is known as long movement.

We have to note that, like the NP movement, each of these movements leaves a trace behind. This is very significant as the traces also play a role in the sentence's syntactical construction and grammaticality.

Before moving to trace-related issues, it is necessary to note the difference between the movements in direct and indirect questions at this juncture.

i. He asked when the principal would come.

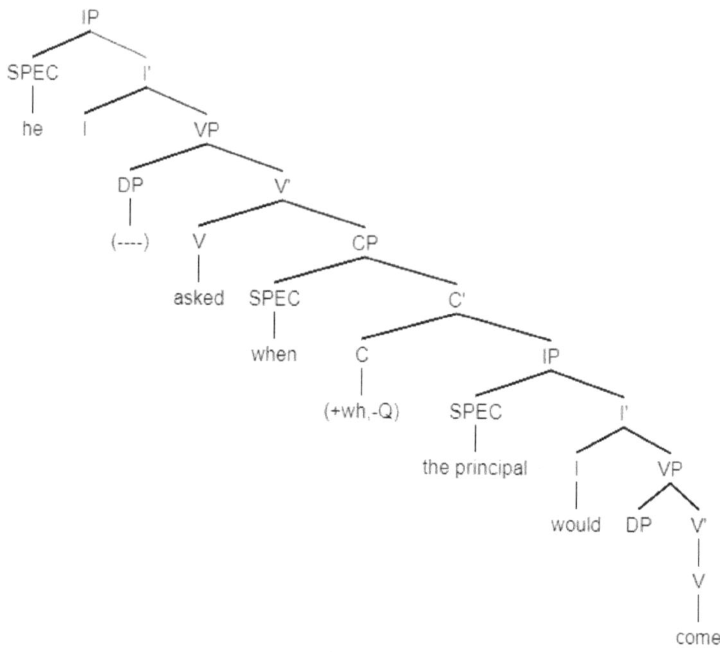

It is worth noting that the wh-Q elements bring the 'when' to the Spec position of CP but prevent the 'would' from moving from the inflection node to the COMP position as there is no +Q element involved. In contrast to direct question formation, there is no auxiliary subject inversion or do-support.

WH - traces

j. I thought that Mr. John might invite many childhood friends.

k. Who do you think Mr. John may invite?

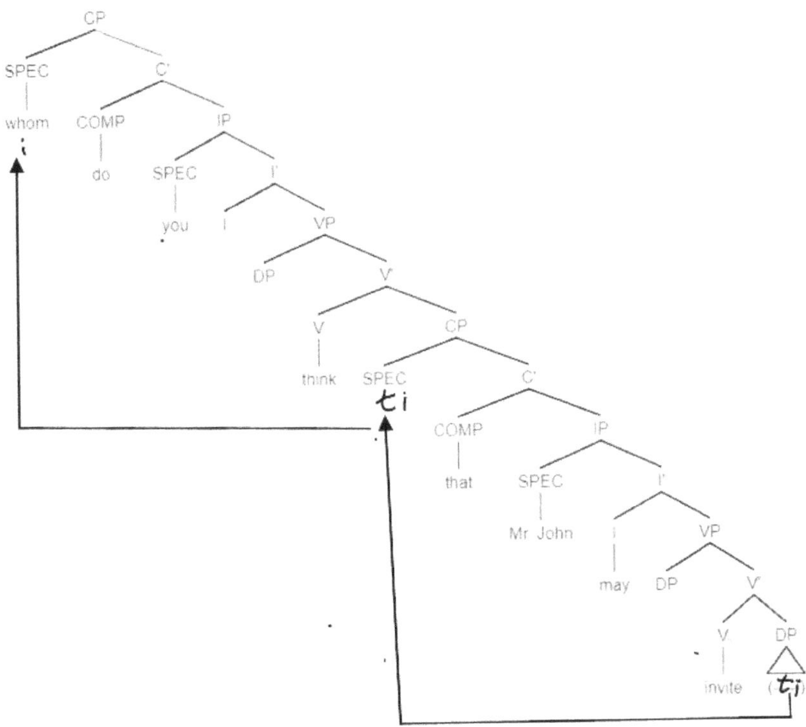

As we have come to know, every movement leaves a trace that fulfils certain functions that are not possible for the moved element from the landing site. Here, in the given example, the DP 'whom' moves from an argument location to the COMP of the CP, which is outside of its domain. The landing location does not have a verb to allocate the theta-role or case. In such a scenario, the traces can meet the requirements of the case filter and the theta criterion. It is impossible to retrieve the accusative case of 'whom' at the landing site because it is missing. However, the trace left behind by the moved phrase can fulfil this necessity accordingly to maintain the grammaticality of the sentence.

THE ISLAND CONSTRAINTS

We discussed long Wh-movements and observed that they leave traces behind to perform certain functions independently. As regards long movements, they are unbounded, as the recursive properties allow any number of CP-clauses in a sentence.

i. $[_{CP}$ What were they building $_{it}]$?

ii. $[_{CP}$ What did he say $[_{CP}$ that they were building $_{ti}]]$?

iii. $[_{CP}$ What $_{i}$ did she claim $[_{CP}$ that he said $[_{CP}$ that they were building $_{ti}]]]$?

iv. $[_{CP}$ What$_{i}$ did you think $[_{CP}$ that she claimed $[_{CP}$ that he said $[_{CP}$ that they were building $_{ti}]]]]$?

v. $[_{CP}$ What $_{i}$ do we believe $[_{CP}$ that you thought $[_{CP}$ that he said $[_{CP}$ that they were building $_{ti}]]]]]$?

The above-mentioned examples show that long-distance Wh-movements are unbounded. In 1967, Ross J discovered that specific phrases are not suitable for extracting to form a Wh-movement, which is known as Island constraints. They are complex NP constraints, coordinate structure constraints, sentential subject constraints, and left branch conditions.

1. **Complex NP constraints.**

   a. He claimed that he had met the prime minister.

   b. *[Who $_{i}$ did he make the claim [that he met $_{ti}$]]?

   c. He revealed the fact that he belonged to a spy network.

   d. *[What$_{i}$ did he reveal the fact that he belonged to $_{ti}$]]?

Sentences b and d are ungrammatical because a DP from a complex NP cannot be moved to another matrix clause SPEC CP.

It is possible to observe the distinction if the clauses are not complex NP clauses but rather CP clauses.

a. He claimed that he met the prime minister.

b. [$_{CP}$ Who $_{I}$ did he claim [$_{CP}$ that he met $_{ti}$]]?

c. He revealed that he belonged to the spy network.

d. [What $_{i}$ did he reveal [that he belonged to $_{ti}$]]?

Coordinate structure constraints.

a. Gita sang a tribal song, and Raju danced well.

b. * Which song did Gita sing and Raju dance well?

c. * How did Raju dance and Gita sing a tribal song?

Any attempt to extract a phrase from a coordinate structure for a Wh-question formation ends up in ungrammaticality.

Sentential subject constraints: He established a novel institution, which is a great success story.

a. *What $_{i}$ has that he established $_{ti}$ is a great success story?

In this example, we tried to extract something from the sentential subject for a prohibited question movement. The name given to this island, which is known as one of the 'Wh-islands,' is sentential subject constraints.

A. Mann read Arundhathi Roy's novel.

B. * Whose $_{i}$ did Mann read $_{ti}$ novel?

C. Whose $_{i}$ novel did Mann read $_{ti}$?

Wh-movement in sentence B is ungrammatical as the left branch condition is violated. However, sentence C is grammatical as the whole NP is involved in the Wh-movement. When a WH-phrase is substituted for the entire complex NP and moved to form a question, this is known as a **pied piping** movement.

Synopsis of the Chapter

Movements in Generative Grammar have undergone significant refinement following the development of the X-bar theory, Principles and Parameters (P&P) theory and Government and Binding (GB) theory. Movements based on different rules under Transformational Generative Grammar (TGG) are now unified under a single framework governed by universal principles such as the Theta Criterion, Case Filter, and Projection Principles. This development made it easy to explain all sorts of movements under a single set of rules, as syntactic issues such as question formation, topicalisation, passivisation, and relativisation ensure grammaticality.

1. Transformations as Movements

When we see movements in the new perspective of Generative grammar, the main difference is that the reasons and causes behind them are almost the same. If we sum up all in the updated framework,

- Movements are syntactic operations where elements are displaced to fulfil structural or interpretive requirements.
- These movements are unified under principles ensuring the preservation of core grammatical conditions:
- Theta Criterion: Ensures arguments are assigned exactly one theta role.
- Case Filter: Ensures all noun phrases are assigned case.
- Projection Principles: Lexical properties are preserved throughout derivation.
- Extended Projection Principle (EPP): Sentences must have subjects, even if implied.

2. Movements in Yes/No Questions

- Process: In yes/no questions, the auxiliary or modal in the Inflectional (I) node moves to the Complementiser (COMP) position at the beginning of the sentence to mark the interrogative nature.
- Example:
- Declarative: "John is happy."
- Interrogative: "Is John happy?"
- Trace: A trace (t) is left in the moved element's original position, linking the surface and deep structures.
- Example: "Is John happy?" → [C Is] [IP John [I t] happy].
- Movement to COMP ensures that the syntactic structure reflects the sentence's interrogative function.

3. Wh-Movements

- Definition: Wh-movement displaces interrogative or relative elements (e.g., "what," "who") to the Specifier of CP position for question or focus formation.
- Examples:
- Declarative: "John ate something."
- Interrogative: "What did John eat?"
- The Wh-word "what" moves to the front of the sentence.
- Trace: The original position of the displaced wh-word is marked by a The wh-word.
- Example: "What did John eat t?"
- Significance of Trace:
- Traces maintain the link between the displaced element and its original theta position, ensuring grammatical coherence.

4. Inflectional Node Movement to COMP

- Reason for Movement:
- The COMP position governs clause type (e.g., declarative, interrogative) and serves as a landing site for inflectional elements.
- Example: In "Did John leave?", the auxiliary "did" moves to COMP to signal the question structure.
- Role in Clause Embedding:
- The COMP node introduces subordinate clauses and governs relationships between main and embedded clauses.

5. Island Constraints

- Definition: Island constraints restrict the domains from which elements can be extracted during movement.
- Types of Islands:

    1. Wh-Island: Prevents extraction from a clause introduced by a wh-word.

- Example: "Who wonders [whether John ate what]?"

(Ungrammatical: "What does who wonder whether John ate?")

    1. Complex NP Island: Restricts movement from within a noun phrase.

- Example: "The book [that John read]"

(Ungrammatical: "What did the book that John read t discuss?")

    1. Adjunct Island: Disallows extraction from adjunct clauses.

- Example: "John left [because he was angry]"

(Ungrammatical: "Why did John leave because he was angry?")

- Purpose of Island Constraints: Prevent ungrammatical extractions that disrupt sentence structure.

6. Importance of Movements in Generative Grammar

- Unified Framework: Movements are now explained under general principles rather than disparate transformations.
- Role of Trace: Traces link displaced elements to their original positions, preserving thematic roles and syntactic relations.
- Cross-Linguistic Applicability: Movements and constraints explain variations in syntax across languages while maintaining a universal grammar framework.
- Interaction with Functional Categories: Movements to COMP or Specifier positions demonstrate the importance of functional projections like IP and CP in sentence structure.

Conclusion

Movements in generative grammar within the frameworks of Government and Binding theory became more principled and cohesive by unifying them under a single set of rules, such as the Case Filter, Theta Criterion, and Projection Principles. This increased the interpretability of movements like question formation, passivisation, relativisation and topicalisation. Furthermore, this demonstrates the interaction between IP and CP with greater clarity and efficiency. The inclusion of trace and the enforcement of island constraints safeguard structural integrity, making movements a cornerstone of modern generative grammar.

CHAPTER VII

MINIMALIST PROGRAMME

So far, we have discussed various development stages of Generative Grammar and how this approach has revolutionised language learning and grammar. We should now discuss the Minimalist Programme and its recent developments, including their effects on grammar and language comprehension.

Even though there have been criticisms and disagreements at various levels, language learning can only proceed with the essential concepts of generative grammar, as introduced by Chomsky. It would be more beneficial if we summarise the language theories and frameworks that align with generative grammar before proceeding to the Minimalist Programme (MP).

Although there are many languages on the Earth, they are mainly thought to have been created by humans. The structure of all languages has something universal to say. Universality lies with languages not only because of the concept that language is an evolutionary by-product of humankind but also because of its structural, social, and other aspects. In many ways, the theories or frameworks of generative grammar can uncover or validate the universality of languages.

The Minimalist Program is a straightforward attempt to use language theories to simplify and enhance its efficiency or reduce grammaticality to a minimum. Considering our previous discussion, a summary of understanding generative grammar would be helpful.

1. In all languages, the syntactic structure makes it possible to produce an unlimited amount of legible and comprehensible sentences with limited resources.
2. Language acquisition is a natural human quality, and humans can do it with the help of a set of grammatical frameworks.
3. Competence and performance: Competence refers to the speaker's implicit knowledge of their language, including its rules and structures and their capacity to create and understand it. Performance is defined as the ability to produce and comprehend language based on different concrete situations, such as memory, social context, and cognitive processes.
4. The lexicon is a crucial part of generative grammar. The term 'mental dictionary' describes a dictionary that provides meaning and categorises the syntactic and morphological properties of words.
5. Phrase structure rules are the fundamental methodology used to construct a sentence.
6. Deep structure and surface structure help us understand how a sentence is constructed and later interpreted. Deep structure defines the different abstract levels of representations, such as semantic and syntactic relationships, regardless of how the outcome appears or is pronounced. After many transformations, it becomes a surface structure that can be pronounced or expressed in various ways. In other words, this is the final and phonetic version of the sentence.

7. The next significant topic of discussion in generative grammar is transformations. These allow for the construction of various surface structures from a single deep structure. The same deep structure exists for both active and passive forms of a sentence, and this is true for other transformations, such as question formations.
8. The X-Bar theory enables the parsing of sentences and strengthens GG's universality by providing a universal structure for all types of phrases. According to the theory, every phrase has a head (X), which is dominated by X' as an intermediate node and XP as its maximum projection. Furthermore, it provides not just identical structural forms for different phrases, like noun phrases and verb phrases, but also hierarchical positions for different components that are nested within them. The recursive property of an element in a sentence is easily depicted using this framework.
9. The Principles and Parameters (P&P) state that all languages in the world are built on a set of universal principles for generation and comprehension. This approach states that the ability of humans to acquire language, regardless of its variety, is only possible if the same principles govern the underlying values. Different languages have different parameters that are applied in accordance with local variations, making it easy for a child who acquires the language to recognise them. The use of this framework allows for the understanding and comparison of languages to learn their similarities and differences.
10. Government and binding theory (GB). In this framework, the syntactic structures of human languages are explained using universal principles and language-specific parameters. GB addresses multiple issues that have not yet been addressed or

complicated since the inception of generative grammar. The syntactic study was transformed by GB into a modular system, making it more transparent and accessible to understand the relationships between each module in a sentence. The modules of X-Bar theory, Theta theory, Case theory, Binding theory, Government theory, Bounding theory, and control theory were characterised by clear syntactic and semantic connections. The popularity of Universal Grammar increased after GB, as it simplified syntactic representations, minimising transformations and constraints.

MINIMALIST PROGRAMME

So far, so good; now, the time has come to discuss the Minimalist Programme, the newest version of Generative Grammar theory. Before that, we have to introduce a set of terminology and abstract concepts to understand it better.

One day, I came across an old friend in a coffee shop. We started talking about subjects that we found interesting and naturally moved on to discussing Generative Grammar and Chomsky. While it was going on, my friend's remarks on minimalist theory struck me for a moment. He stated, 'Chomsky built a tower of grammar theories, but suddenly, like a small child in a nursery class, he dismantled it, saying he wanted to build a new, simplest one." "This is what I understood about his new programme."

Although it was meant as a joke, many people consider Chomsky to have broken down all theories in order to construct a new one. Let's have a thorough discussion before concluding.

Before the introduction of the minimalist program, Noam Chomsky began to discuss two concepts: descriptive adequacy and explanatory adequacy. We will have a short discussion before proceeding. Both concepts are a scrutinising mechanism of grammar theories. Descriptive adequacy describes something in detail, whereas explanatory adequacy explains why it is so. For example, there is a big house, and one can explain its good and bad features, such as how many rooms it has, how ventilated they are, which way one could escape in case of a fire, etc. This can be extended to every single detail. We call this phenomenon descriptive adequacy. Coming to explanatory adequacy, it explains why the building is located there, why and how each room is planned, in what way the escape route is constructed... In such a way, it can point out the reason and cause behind each feature. The first one explains the entity in its present state, similar to conducting an inquest, and the second one performs a postmortem. If I say it in a different way, videography is the first choice, and blueprint is the second choice.

Both tools were employed to evaluate the earlier versions of generative theories. For example, the GB theory achieved descriptive adequacy by engaging different modules such as government theory, binding theory, theta theory, case theory, and control theory. The Principles and Parameters theory has been utilised to achieve explanatory adequacy, for instance, by explaining that pro-drop language is a language-specific phenomenon. We must see how both perceive the MP, but before that, we will discuss specific new terms related to the MP.

Language faculty:

The idea is that the language facility is an optimally designed component of the human brain that manages the computational processes of language construction and comprehension. The development of this is both a physiological development as a cognitive capability and a natural achievement as an evolutionary byproduct. In terms of previous versions of theoretical frameworks such as GB, Language faculty is defined as a rich Universal Grammar with innate Principles and parameters. However, it has now been redefined as a simpler mechanism of language construction called Merge.

Logical Form (LF) and Phonological Form (PF)

For various reasons, the Minimalist Programme discarded the frameworks of Deep Structure and Surface Structure and substituted them with LF and PF. These are the two kinds of derivational levels for interpreting a sentence in the MP.

LF serves as the interface for meaning (semantics), and PF serves as the interface for pronunciation (phonetics). Meaning is determined by the interpretation of syntactic structures at the LF level, which determines the syntactic relations of specifiers, complements, adjuncts, and binding elements such as anaphors and pronouns. The LF level also interprets the movements that impact meaning.

The PF connects syntax and phonology. It is responsible for determining word order, phonetic realisation, and prosody. Movements that impact pronunciation occur in this area.

By removing the concepts of deep structure and surface structure, sentence construction becomes much simpler through Merge instead of using pre-determined levels of interpretation.

Merge

In the Minimalist Programme (MP), Merge becomes the prime syntactic operation that constructs all sorts of hierarchical structures, combining smaller units into larger ones. It avoids all intermediate nodes that we have seen earlier to make syntactical and semantic functions the simplest and most unavoidable. There are two types of Merge: external and internal; external merge connects two components to form a phrase, while internal Merge involves re-merging the phrases or moving the components from one place to another.

MP relies on the single syntactic operation, Merge, to simplify sentence construction and avoid all complexities.

Move

Move is another essential operation in MP that Merge follows. The internal Move discussed earlier is actually referred to as Merge. Move's primary purpose is to meet syntactic constraints, such as feature checking and the External Projection Principle (MPP).

Feature Checking

Feature checking is the fundamental mechanism to ensure the well-formedness of a sentence by adhering to its grammatical constraints.

Agree

Agree is the term used for the mechanism to establish a relationship between matching features. It depends on the Probe and goal to interpret features like agreement, tense, and case. Those elements that are interpretable are accepted, and those that are not deleted.

Probe and goal

The probe is an uninterpretable element, whereas the goal is interpretable. The operation Agree depends on these two for feature checking. Once a probe locates a goal in a sentence, the matching features are checked to ensure that grammatical rules are followed. If the features don't match, the probe is deleted at the LF level.

The Minimalist Program (MP) is a continuous significant development in generative grammar, integrating and refining concepts introduced in earlier frameworks. The progression consists of essential insights into language architecture, starting with the lexicon and proceeding to phrase structure, X-bar theory, principles and parameters, and Government and Binding (GB) theory. This paved the way for MP, which prioritises simplicity and efficiency in linguistic computation, presentation, and imposition of grammaticality with ease.

The lexicon, as introduced in earlier theories, was essential in comprehending how words influence syntactic structures. Lexical items were both carriers of meaning and repositories of syntactic and morphological features. For example, the verb eat in John eats an apple carries features that determine its requirement for a subject and an object. These features in the Minimalist Program are considered to be central to the computational process, particularly in the feature-checking mechanism.

The development of phrase structure rules resulted in X-bar theory, which gave a consistent framework for creating syntactic phrases like NP (Noun Phrase), VP (Verb Phrase), and AP (Adjective Phrase). For instance, a sentence like A dog chased the cat can be represented in X-bar terms, showing hierarchical relationships like Specifier (the), Head (dog/chased), and Complement (the cat). The Minimalist Program simplifies these structures by substituting phrase-specific rules with a single, generalised operation known as Merge, which recursively blends elements to create bigger structures.

The Principles and Parameters (P&P) framework transformed linguistic theory by establishing universal principles that govern all languages and a set of parameters that vary across languages. For example, the Head Parameter explains why English places heads (verbs) before complements (He eats rice), while Malayalam places them after (അവൻ ചോറ് കഴിക്കുന്നു [avan choru kazhikkunnu]). The Minimalist Program retains its cross-linguistic emphasis but simplifies it to fundamental computational properties, elucidating parametric variation because of feature specifications in lexical items.

The introduction of modularity into syntactic theory by Government and Binding (GB) theory resulted in the organisation of phenomena such as case assignment and pronoun reference into distinct modules. For example, in John likes himself, GB explains the reflexive himself through binding principles. In the Minimalist Program, the focus is on how syntactic structures satisfy interface conditions with minimal computational effort while also reinterpreting these modules in terms of economic principles.

Considering the insights of previous theories, the Minimalist Program aims to create a more unified and parsimonious explanation of linguistic phenomena. MP provides a simplified framework that accounts for the same linguistic patterns with fewer theoretical assumptions by prioritising economy and reducing redundancy. For example, the derivation of 'the cat chased the mouse' can now be explained through a series of efficient computational steps, from lexical feature selection to the application of Merge and agreement mechanisms. The progression reflects the main objective of generative grammar: uncovering the optimal design of the Language Faculty.

The Minimalist Program (MP) is a result of the transition from Government and Binding (GB) theory to the Minimalist Program (MP), which emphasises theoretical economy instead of descriptive richness within generative grammar. The Minimalist Programme sought to simplify this framework by emphasising economy and optimality. MP retained the core insights of GB but reinterpreted them under the premise that language operates as an efficient computational system driven by minimal resources and constrained by interface conditions. The shift is a larger initiative to uncover the essential characteristics of the human language faculty in accordance with the principles of cognitive and biological economy.

ECONOMY OF DERIVATION

According to this principle, derivations must involve as few steps as possible to produce a grammatically acceptable sentence. Feature checking or interface requirements necessitate the use of syntactic operations like Merge and Move only when necessary. For example, moving a subject to Spec-TP (specifier of Tense Phrase) is done solely for checking the EPP (Extended Projection Principle) feature or for case assignment.

Example:

Derivation of the sentence John eats an apple involves:

- Merging eats with an apple to form a VP.
- Merging the VP with T (tense) to form a TP.
- Moving John to Spec-TP to satisfy the EPP feature.

Tree Diagram:

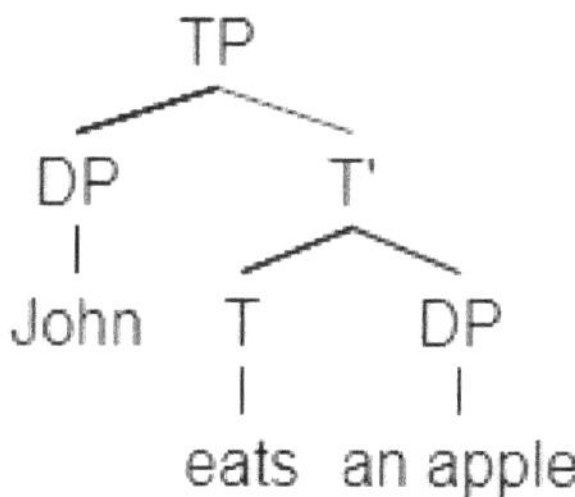

ECONOMY OF REPRESENTATION

This principle aims to reduce the representation to a minimum, avoiding unnecessary nodes and intermediate nodes and keeping only those needed for interpretation. This aids in eliminating redundancy. Functional projections such as TP and CP are necessary to express grammatical relationships and ensure interpretability.

For example, in the derivation of "Who did John see?" To form the question and satisfy its structure, "who" moves to the Spec-CP.

These principles embody the minimalist objective of simplifying syntactic derivations to the most crucial elements and operations, emphasising the language faculty's inherent efficiency.

Interface Conditions: Syntax, Semantics, and Phonology

The Minimalist Program defines syntax as a computational system that works with two interface levels, namely LF and PF, to guarantee that linguistic structures are interpretable. Interface conditions that linguistic expressions must meet are imposed by these interfaces that connect syntax with semantics and phonology, respectively.

LOGICAL FORM (LF)

Syntax-Semantics Interface

LF is the level at which syntactic structures are interpreted for their semantic content. The LF operations make sure that structures are semantically coherent and interpretable. For example, movement operations such as wh-movement or quantifier raising occur to align with semantic requirements.

Example:

In the question What did John eat? to ensure the correct interpretation of LF as a question, it is recommended to move the 'wh' word to the front of the sentence in syntax. In LF, the question is interpreted meaningfully by maintaining the relationship between what and the verb eat.

Representation at LF:

LF: [What [did John eat __]?]

The original position of what is indicated by the trace (_) is to preserve its syntactic relationship for semantic interpretation.

PHONOLOGICAL FORM (PF)

Syntax-Phonology Interface

The PF level is concerned with transferring syntactic structures to phonetic representations for articulation. PF's operations ensure that language structures comply with phonological rules. Some of the tasks that need to be done include word order adjustments, deleting unpronounced elements, and stress assignments.

Example:

Syntactic operations, like subject-verb agreement in John Loves Mary, must be completed before the structure is linearised at PF for pronunciation. At PF, features such as case (nominative for John) are not spoken, but they have a significant influence on the final word order.

Representation at PF:

PF: [John loves Mary]

3. Syntax as the Mediator

LF and PF receive hierarchical structures generated by Syntax, which serves as the computational core. These structures must meet the requirements of both interfaces.

- At LF, the structures must be semantically interpretable, meaning all features, such as tense, case, and scope, are resolved.
- At PF, structures must comply with phonological constraints, which ensures well-formedness for articulation.

Example of Interface Workflow:

For the sentence Whom did John see?:

- Syntax: Generates the structure of those who moved to Spec-CP for question formation.
- LF: LF interprets who as the object of the verb in a semantic question.
- PF: Linearises the structure for pronunciation, ensuring appropriate word order and stress.

Tree Diagram Linking Syntax, LF, and PF:

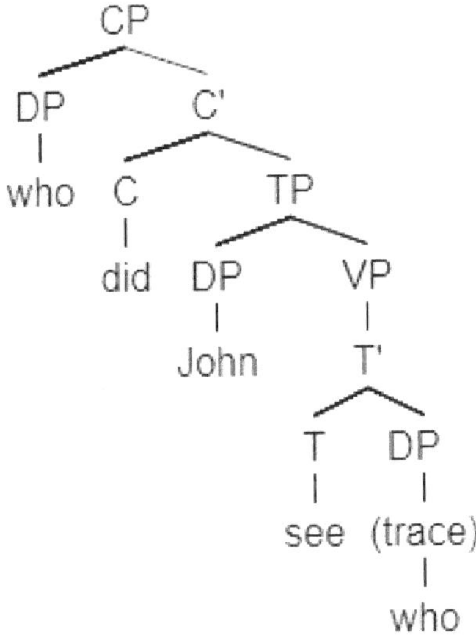

LF: [Who [did John see _]?]

PF: [Who did John see?]

The Minimalist Program uses LF and PF to ensure that syntactic computation outputs are meaningful and pronounceable and adhere to the interface conditions necessary for human language.

LANGUAGE FACULTY

The language faculty was built on the belief that human beings have the unique ability to learn and use language, which is a characteristic of our species. According to Chomsky, the human brain has a specialised system called Universal Grammar (UG) that is responsible for the foundation of all human languages. This system enables us to create and comprehend an infinite number of sentences through the use of a limited set of rules and words.

The Minimalist Program expands on this concept by suggesting that the language faculty be designed to be as uncomplicated and efficient as possible. The argument is that language is an efficient computational system, which means it uses the least amount of effort to create structures that are both meaningful (for communication) and pronounceable (for articulation). The effectiveness is evident in the way the syntactic system interacts with two interfaces: Logical Form (LF) for meaning and Phonological Form (PF) for sound.

This design reflects the cognitive evolution of humans as a species from an evolutionary perspective. Humans' brains evolved to efficiently process complex information, including the ability to combine ideas and concepts in creative ways. Language is responsible for making this possible. The Minimalist Program emphasises that language structure reflects evolutionary adaptations, with a focus on simplicity and optimality in speech processing and production.

The Human Language Faculty is not only based on biology but also designed to meet the cognitive demands of communication while reducing effort, as suggested by Chomsky's ideas and the Minimalist Program. This reflects a sophisticated evolutionary advancement.

MINIMALIST SYNTAX, MERGE & MOVE

The Minimalist Program's central concept is minimalist syntax, which focuses on how the human language faculty generates grammatical sentences through simple, efficient operations. The language system must meet two interface requirements: Logical Form (LF) and Phonological Form. (LF) stands for semantic interpretation, while PF stands for phonological ends. Merge and Move, which are essential for constructing syntactic structures in a minimalist framework, are responsible for adhering to these conditions.

Merge: Building Structures

Unlike the frameworks we discussed earlier, Merge is the term used to process and bring two elements (words or phrases) together to form a single hierarchical structure in minimalist syntax. From the viewpoint of this syntactical structure, Merge is considered a simple but straightforward tool for building recursive structures characteristic of human language

Let us see now how Merge works, for example, in the sentence John eats apples:

- ➢ The verb eats is merged with the noun phrase apples to form the verb phrase (VP):

[VP eats apples]

- ➢ The subject John is merged with the VP to form the complete sentence (TP):

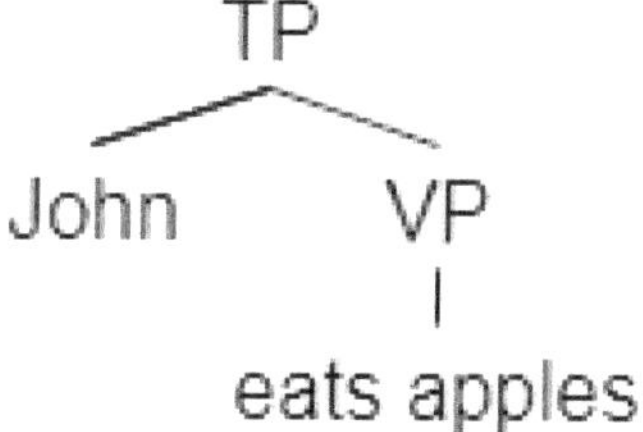

[TP John [VP eats apples]]

By carrying out this operation, the structure can be interpreted as a meaningful sentence at LF and linearised at PF (which is pronounceable).

Move: Ensuring Grammaticality

Move is the operation that repositions elements within the structure to satisfy grammatical or interface requirements, such as subject-verb agreement, case assignment, or forming questions. It allows language to maintain grammatical relationships while meeting the demands of LF and PF.

- Example of Move:

In a question like What does John eat?

- The object that starts in the VP:

[VP eat what]

- To form a question, what moves to the beginning of the sentence (Spec-CP) to satisfy the requirements of LF for question interpretation:

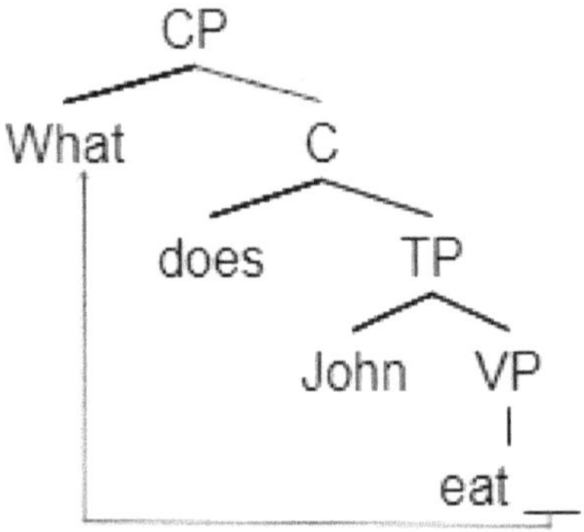

[CP What [C does [TP John [VP eat __]]]]

Adherence to LF and PF

Both operations, Merge and Move, ensure that the structure meets the needs of the two interfaces:

- At LF: The structure must be interpretable for meaning. For instance, by moving what, the sentence can be understood as a question.

- At PF, the structure must be pronounceable. For example, in 'What does John eat?', to satisfy English phonology requirements, the auxiliary is inserted at PF.

Minimalist Design and Language Faculty

The efficiency of the human language faculty can be seen in the use of Merge and Move. These minimal yet powerful operations help the syntactical structure adhere to interface conditions and construct complex sentences. In Chomsky's idealistic view of language, minimalist syntax conforms to sentence construction and becomes effortless, eloquent, and balanced when it comes to computation. The concepts of Merge and Move are the core innate machinery of the human mind in the Minimalist Programme (MP), which helps to create limitless language expressions with minimal complexity. This reflects Chomsky's strong desire to integrate the structural mechanisms of all languages into a universal perspective.

Feature Checking and the Role of Agree

Agree is the other new term introduced for feature checking of syntactic structures that work as a unit after the Merge and Move operations. The Minimalist Program relies on feature checking and Agree to ensure that grammatical structures are well-formed. The matching of features like tense, number, and case leads to the resolution of relationships between elements in a sentence, such as subjects, verbs, and objects, using these concepts. The Minimalist framework recognises Agree as a formal operation, but it differs from the broader grammatical idea of agreement, which focuses on observable patterns in sentences.

Feature Checking: Ensuring Grammaticality

Nouns, verbs, and functional heads are examples of elements that carry features in syntax

- The phi features (φ) include a person, number, and gender.
- The features of a case are Nominative, accusative, and so on.
- Past, present, and progressive are all tense and aspect features.

The derivation process requires feature checking to ensure that these features are matched and 'checked'.

For example:

- The subject must match the person and number characteristics of the verb (He runs in contrast to They run).
- It is necessary for a noun to verify case features that include functional heads, such as T (Tense) or v (little v, which is a functional projection in the verb phrase).

If the features are not checked, the derivation fails, indicating that the structure is ungrammatical.

The Role of Agree: A Minimalist Operation

The Minimalist framework uses 'Agree' as a formal syntactic operation to verify features. An association is made between a functional head (referred to as the probe) and another element (referred to as the goal).

Syntactic dependencies are established in agreement and movement operations through the probe-goal system in the minimalist approach to generative grammar. A probe is an element (typically a functional head, such as Tense or v) that has uninterpretable or unvalued features and actively searches for a matching goal, an element (such as a noun or verb) that carries the required interpretable or valued features. Once the probe finds the goal in its accessible domain (its c-command domain), it establishes a relationship of agreement and values its features accordingly. Syntactic well-formedness requires this operation to ensure that structures comply with feature-checking principles. The probe-goal interaction reduces derivational complexity by eliminating unnecessary steps and preserving linguistic economy in computations, which is in line with the broader objectives of the Minimalist Program.

Now, we will see how Agree operates.

1. Probe and Goal Relationship:
   - A probe, such as T or v, seeks a compatible goal (like a noun or pronoun) in the structure to evaluate its features.
   - The goal should be within the probe's domain (within its c-command range) and contain features that are not important but can be matched with the probe.
2. **Mechanics of Agree**:
   - The probe initiates Agree to fix unappreciated features on both elements.
   - For example, in She runs, the T head contains unrecognised φ-features (person and number) that are valued by the subject She via Agree.
3. **Example in Syntax:**
   - In the sentence, John eats an apple.
   - The T head (tense) is the probe and has unvalued φ features.
   - The subject John is the goal, providing person and number features.
   - Agree to ensure that these features match and satisfy the grammatical requirements.

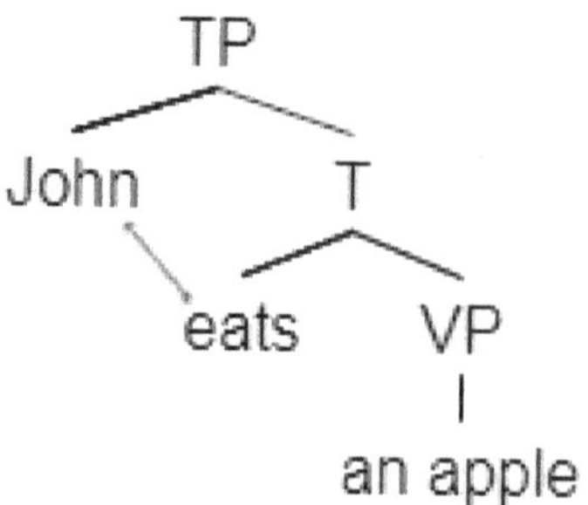

[TP John [T eats [VP an apple]]]

Agree vs. General Grammatical Term "Agreement"

Although related, the term 'agree' in Minimalist syntax is not the same as the general definition of agreement.

1. Agree (Formal Syntactic Operation):

- A technical process in which features are matched and verified between a probe and a goal.
- It is not visible to surface representation and is a component of the computational system.

2. Agreement (Observable Phenomenon):

- It is the alignment of features in a sentence that can be seen.
- Examples:
- Subject-verb agreement (She runs vs. They run).
- Subject-verb agreement (అతను వెళ్తాడు "He goes" vs. వాళ్లు వెళ్తారు "They go" in Telugu).

3. Key Difference:

- Agree operates as an underlying mechanism to ensure feature alignment in Minimalist syntax; it is invisible and limited to LF.

- The agreement is the grammatical pattern of a language's surface realisation of alignment that is visible at the pronunciation level.

Adherence to LF and PF

- In Logical Form (LF), Agree is responsible for ensuring semantic coherence by assigning case and scope to elements correctly.
- At the phonological level, surface agreement patterns are determined by Agree, which makes the sentence pronounceable and grammatical.

The Minimalist Program simplifies its approach to describing agreement phenomena by prioritising Agree as a computational mechanism. This provides efficiency and optimality, reducing complexity and avoiding redundancy.

PHASES AND CYCLIC DERIVATIONS

Phases and cyclic derivations are the next important concepts in the Minimalist Program. These fundamental ideas simplify syntactic processing, making it easier to construct sentences incrementally. The step-by-step architecture is made manageable on a local basis and structural well-formedness is guaranteed by the Language Faculty through modular sentence generation through phases. The use of these concepts is in line with computational parsimony, which allows for phrase-by-phrase composition instead of requiring analysis of the sentence as a whole.

Phases and cyclic derivations are the next essential topics for the Minimalist Programme. These fundamental concepts streamline syntactic computation, making it easier. They generate sentences in smaller chunks known as phases, making the construction manageable locally and ensuring well-formedness for the Language Faculty. The use of these concepts aligns with the principles of computational economy, which allows for incremental derivation of sentences instead of processing the entire structure at once.

Phases: Chunks of Derivation

A phase, or 'chunk', is a unit or sequence of words that marks a natural point in the derivation when a portion of the text is finished and sent to the interfaces of Logical Form (LF) and Phonological Form (PF). Chomsky's phase theory simplifies syntactic computation by dividing it into smaller, independently interpretable units.

1. Phase Heads:

   The phase heads are designated for specific functional heads, including v (little v, in the verb phrase) and C (complementiser, in the clause). Marking the boundaries of phases is how they control their completion. (In the Minimalist Program, the little v (vP) is used as a functional head when it introduces an external argument and assigns an agent or causer role in transitive and unergative constructions.)

2. Phase Impenetrability Condition (PIC):

   According to the PIC, once a phase is finished, its internal structure is not accessible for syntactic operations except for the material at its 'edge'. (e.g., the specifier or head). This ensures that only essential information is kept for further calculations, which reduces redundancy.

Example of a Phase:

- In the sentence, John thinks Mary left: The Verb Phrase (VP) and Complementiser Phrase (CP) are phases:

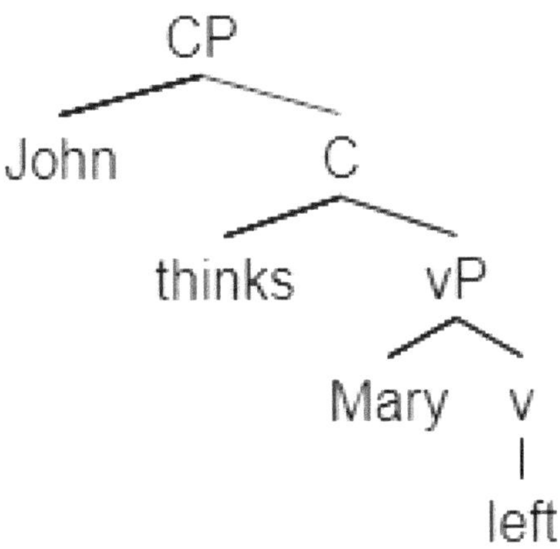

[CP John [C thinks [vP Mary [v left]]]]

- When the vP phase is finished, it is sent to LF and PF for interpretation, and then the subsequent phase (CP) commences.

Cyclic Derivations: Step-by-Step Construction

We have seen how operations like Merge and Move construct sentences with limited and simpler complexity in their domain and how the process Agree checks features to make sentences acceptable. Then, we saw how phases made the chunks of sentences compatible with the Language Faculty. Now, we will discuss how Cyclic Derivations proceed by systematically analysing the syntactic structure of complex sentences part by part, avoiding the complexity of extracting the whole sentence at once.

1. **Building in Cycles**:

   - The structure for each phase is finalised and sent to the interfaces before the next phase starts.
   - The use of this cyclic process eliminates the need for long-distance computations by checking features locally in each phase.

2. **Cyclic Movement:**

   In order to meet the Phase Impenetrability Condition, elements like 'wh' words (such as who, what) move across multiple phases in steps, stopping at the end of each phase.

Example of Cyclic Movement:

- In the sentence What did John say Mary ate?
- What moves from its original position in the lower vP to the edge of the CP phase and then to the main clause CP:

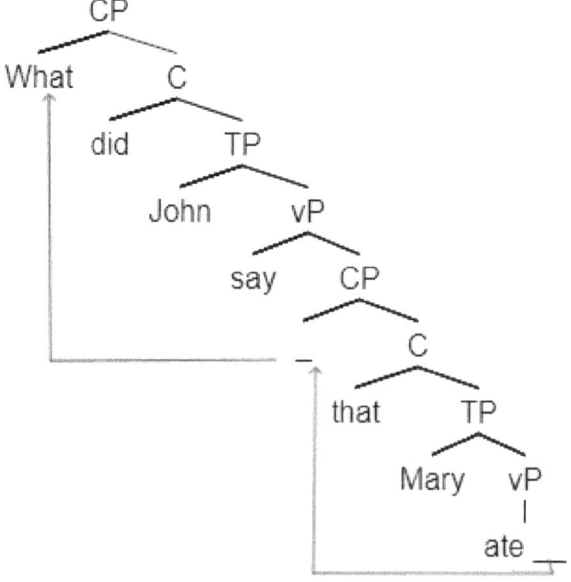

[CP What [C did [TP John [vP say [CP _ [C that [TP Mary [vP _ ate __]]]]]]]]

Detailed Interaction Between Phases and Cyclic Derivations

1. Deriving the Sentence "Who does John think left?"

   - Phase 1 (vP): The subject who is merged and checked for case in the embedded vP phase:

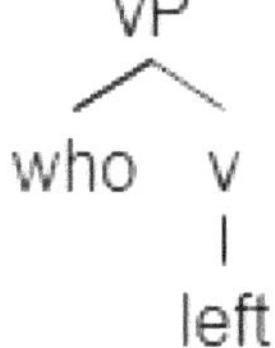

Phase 1: [vP who [v left]]

- Once completed, the vP phase is sent to the interfaces.
- In Phase 2, who moves to the edge of the embedded CP to meet Wh-movement requirements.

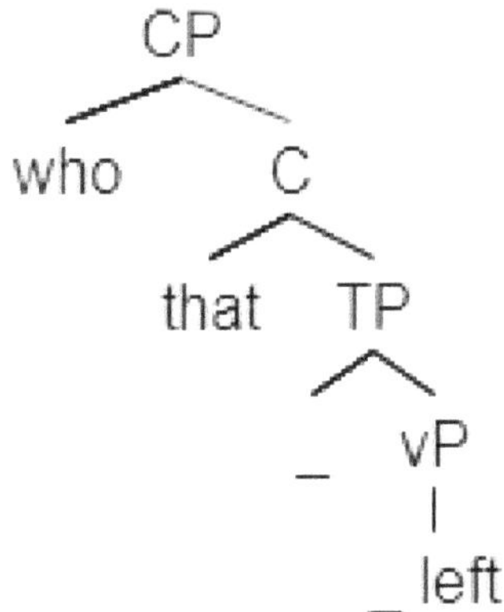

Phase 2: [CP who [C that [TP _ [vP _ left]]]]

➢ In Phase 3 (Main CP): Who moves to the main CP phase for question formation:

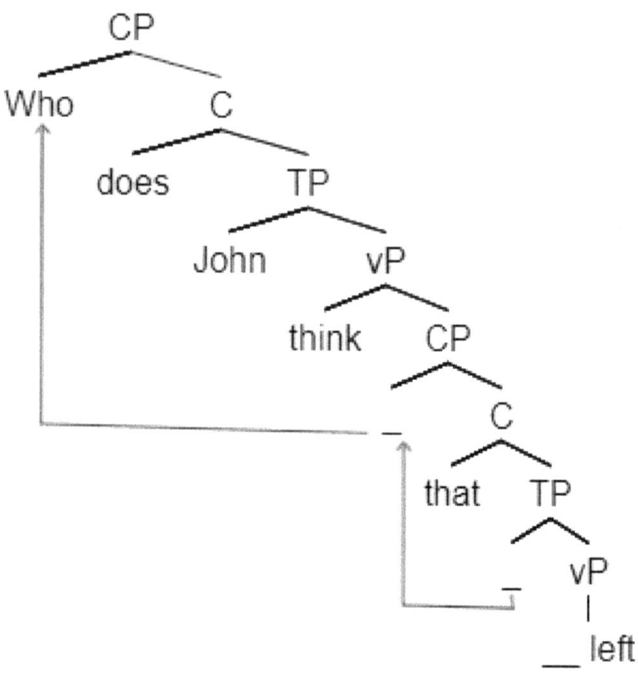

Phase 3: [CP Who [C does [TP John [vP think [CP _ [C that [TP _ [vP _ left]]]]]]]]

2. **Advantages of Cyclic Derivations and Phases:**

   ➢ The sentence structure is divided into phases, which reduces the need for computation to build the structure piece by piece rather than the entire sentence.

   ➢ The scope of ungrammatical derivation errors can be limited by locality by allowing structures such as movement and agreement to apply in constrained domains

- In order to ensure compatibility, all phases are interpreted incrementally through interfaces, resulting in seamless interaction with LF and PF

In conclusion, the Minimalist Program's innovations of phases and cyclic derivations simplify sentence generation. The language faculty maximises computation and adheres to economic principles by arranging syntax into smaller, interpretable chunks (phases) and building structures step by step (cyclically). These mechanisms demonstrate the effectiveness of human language as a system that balances complexity with ease.

UNIVERSAL GRAMMAR AS REVISED IN MINIMALISM

Noam Chomsky's proposal of universal grammar (UG) serves as the theoretical basis for human language capacity. The theory is that human beings are born with an innate, biologically determined system that provides the basic principles and structures that are universal to all languages. In the Minimalist Program (MP), UG has transformed from earlier frameworks like the Government and Binding (GB) theory to a more elaborate and simplified system. Minimalism builds upon UG by prioritising efficiency, simplicity, and optimal design in the human language faculty.

Universal Grammar (UG) in the Generative Tradition

1. In GB Theory:

- UG was conceived as a comprehensive set of principles and parameters.
- Universal rules, such as the X-bar theory, that are applicable to all languages are known as principles.

- Languages have different parameters that are specific options within the universal framework. (e.g., whether a language allows pro-drop).
- A detailed and modular approach to syntax was provided by UG in GB, which concentrated on areas such as case assignment, theta roles, and binding theory.

2. In the Minimalist programme:

- Despite retaining the core idea of UG, the Minimalist Program aims to simplify its description.
- It raises the question of the need for a UG that is richly detailed. It suggests that most of the linguistic diversity is caused by external factors, like the interaction of UG with other cognitive systems and language-specific rules.

Minimalist Analysis of UG

Economy of Design:

- Minimalism views UG as the 'optimal' design for the language faculty, including only the operations and constraints considered strictly necessary.
- The minimum components needed for UG have been minimised:
- Feature checking and Agree are basic strategies for grammaticality checking with limited computation cost.

2. Redefining Parameters:

- UG does not consider parameters, as we have seen in PP, a part of it. Instead, UG considers the particularities of the lexicon as an external factor in the choice of phonological constraints. (For example, in PP, SOV, and SVO, patterns of sentences are thought to be a language-specific feature, but in UG, they are considered to be a variation of interaction between lexicons of choice.)

Universal Grammar and the Advancement of Generative Grammar

The Minimalist Program reshaped Generative Grammar by redefining Universal Grammar (UG) to focus on economy, simplicity, and optimal design. A richly structured UG with multiple independent modules and constraints was assumed by previous generative models, like Government and Binding Theory (GB). According to the Minimalist Program, UG should solely consist of the most essential and computationally efficient principles. Minimalism prioritises a limited number of crucial operations, such as Merge and Agree, instead of numerous language-specific rules. This change resulted in a more derivational than representational perspective of syntax, with phases serving as local domains for computation. UG was perceived as a compact system that was limited by interface conditions instead of a vast repository of rules. By comparing both GB and MP, the picture will become clearer

1. From GB to MP:

The change from GB to minimalism signifies a transformation in the way UG is conceived.

- GB: The focus was on elucidating the complexity of syntactic phenomena by using detailed modules such as government, binding, and movement rules.
- Minimalism: This approach simplifies these modules, emphasising the general principles and reducing redundancy. It views linguistic phenomena as emerging from a simpler UG that interacts with interface conditions (Logical Form and Phonological Form).

2. Example of UG Simplification:

- In GB, the allocation of cases depended on specific government configurations.
- Minimalism reduces the need for a separate case module by assigning the case through the Agree operation.

Key Features of UG in Minimalism

1. Core Principles of UG:

- The language faculty functions as a computer system that ties syntax to meaning and sound.
- Only essential tools like Merge, Move, and UG provide feature checking for language deriving.

2. Interface Conditions:

Given the interaction of UG with cognitive and articulatory systems, we take it that derivations are only forced to be interpretable at LF and pronounceable at PF.

3. Foundations: Biological and Cognitive

Concerning Chomsky's idea that LF is a genetic endowment, minimalism is very closely tied to that.

Nevertheless, it has evolved along with human cognition; language itself is an economical system with flexibility.

Universal Grammar is rethought in the Minimalist Program as a streamlined, biologically based system that provides the essential set of operations and principles for language. This viewpoint coincides with the shift in generative grammar from the modular and parameter-rich GB framework to a more efficient and straightforward model. Minimalism presents a compelling narrative of how human languages emerge from a universal cognitive foundation while allowing for diversity among linguistic communities by emphasising the interaction between UG and external systems.

MINIMALIST PROGRAMME, EARLY FRAMEWORK AND TREE-ADJOINING GRAMMAR

The Minimalist Program (MP) conceptualises tree generation differently from previous frameworks of generative grammar, like Phrase Structure Grammar, X-bar Theory, and Government and Binding (GB) Theory. In the early frameworks, syntactic trees were generated through complex rules and transformations, with multiple modules addressing different syntactic phenomena. The GB theory used mechanisms like Move-α and modular constraints (e.g., Binding and Case theories) to derive sentence structures.

MP simplifies tree generation by using Merge and Move as the two core operations. These operations result in a uniform mechanism for structure-building and displacement, eliminating the need for multiple transformation rules. For example, through the binary merger, the MP tree for the sentence "John loves Mary" is generated.

[TP John [T' T [vP John [v' loves [VP loves Mary]]]]]

Here, Merge is used hierarchically to combine elements, while Move (if necessary) applies cyclically and adheres to principles such as phases and locality.

Comparison with Early Frameworks

Early Frameworks:

Derivations in GB required the use of pre-specified phrase structure rules and transformational steps such as Move α. For example, in wh-questions (What did John eat?), the wh-element had to undergo multiple specific transformations, each constrained by independent modules.

[CP What [C' did [TP John [vP John [v' eat what]]]]]

Minimalist Program:

MP makes the process easier by combining merge and cyclic movement in accordance with general principles, like agreement and phase impenetrability conditions. By adapting insights from Tree Adjoining Grammar (TAG), the derivation is designed to meet economic and interface requirements.

TAG utilises elementary trees (basic structures) and adjoining operations to extend these trees. Minimalism takes advantage of this recursive perspective through the merge, which builds trees in an iterative and dynamic format.

For example:

- In TAG, John loves Mary begins with an initial tree for the verb 'loves', which is enhanced by noun phrases (John and Mary) adjoining it.
- In MP, Merge iterates by combining lexical items (John, loves, and Mary) to produce a similar hierarchical structure without the need for fixed elementary trees.

Unlike TAG, MP incorporates adjunction-like behaviour into its Merge mechanism, which is defined as a structural operation. Both approaches stress the recursive nature of syntax, but MP creates a single system that aligns with the cognitive economy.

This argument implies that the Minimalist Program refines tree generation by eliminating the need for rigid phrase structure rules and modular constraints and replacing them with universal operations like Merge and Move. MP uses Tree Adjoining Grammar insights to adopt a dynamic and recursive approach for tree construction, which ensures both flexibility and computational efficiency for derivations.

Critiques And Limitations Of Minimalist Programme.

The introduction of the Minimalist Program (MP) in linguistics by Noam Chomsky led to both revolutionary and controversial developments. Though it has attempted to offer a simplification of linguistic theory and to categorise the essential characteristics of the human language faculty, the theory has come under a great deal of criticism from linguists. Critics addressed its theoretical assumptions, empirical sufficiency, and relevance to a larger understanding of language. Some of the more major criticisms and limits that have been raised against MP are shown below, together with notable linguists who have opposed or questioned its claims.

1. Vagueness in the Concept of the Language Faculty

The MP model represents an ideal computational system that critics have accused MP of being too abstract and too untouched from the physical reality of the brain.

- A primary criticism of Chomsky's conception of a language faculty (FL) is that it is claimed to be designed for efficiency and perfection, but this claim lacks biological or cognitive evidence.
- Geoffrey Sampson and Philip Lieberman: 'Language probably evolved according to biological rules, which would have been more concerned with functionality and adaptability

(the resource-constrained world of evolutionary selection) than with computational "optimality" (such as the speed of mathematical proofs)'.

- Sampson asks if FL is inborn and what if structural elements emerge through use and interaction rather than via UG?

2. Lack of Empirical testability and what if structural elements emerge through use and interaction rather than via UG?

MP's reliance on abstract concepts like merge and phases has been criticised as unfalsifiable.

- According to Paul Postal, many of MP's claims cannot be empirically tested because they often redefine phenomena to fit the theory instead of incorporating actual linguistic data
- Critics claim that the emphasis on clear explanations can jeopardise the accuracy of modelling linguistic diversity.

3. Overemphasis on Economy Principles

The MP stresses the importance of economy in derivation and representation (such as Shortest Move and Phase Impenetrability Condition), but these principles are viewed as too simple.

- Frederick Newmeyer brought attention to the fact that human languages often display redundancy and irregularity, which runs counter to the notion of an 'optimal' language faculty.
- Some linguists have asserted that economic principles are theoretical constructs instead of observable facts.

4. Insufficient Attention to Linguistic Variation

- The neglect of cross-linguistic diversity is one of the most significant criticisms of MP.

- Daniel Everett, who is known for his study of the Piraha language, questioned MP's universality by contending that Piraha lacks recursion, which is essential to Chomsky's UG hypothesis. This poses a direct challenge to MP's claim that recursion is an innate feature of all languages.
- Nicholas Evans and Stephen Levinson, among others, have pointed out that there is much more linguistic diversity than MP accounts for, and a theory of Universal Grammar must include this variation.

5. Ignoring Functional and Social Factors

MP has been criticised for separating syntax from functional, social, and cognitive influences.

- According to Michael Tomasello and other linguists, language is a result of social interaction and shared intentions rather than an innate computational system. The idea that syntax is independent of meaning and context is questioned by Tomasello's work in usage-based linguistics. Not only does this perspective illuminate our understanding of language, but it also provides intriguing possibilities for further research and exploration.
- According to critics, the Minimalist Program neglects the significant role of external factors, like cultural evolution and cognitive constraints, in shaping language despite its emphasis on internal computation.

6. Minimalist Assumptions and Biological Plausibility

The minimalist argument that language is 'perfectly designed' to communicate has been challenged on biological grounds.

- According to Philip Lieberman, human language is not a perfect system but rather a product of evolutionary compromises caused by limitations in anatomy and neural processing.

- Scholars who assert that Merge is a unique and defining characteristic of the human language faculty have questioned the notion that similar operations are present in other cognitive systems.

7. Theoretical Complexity Disguised as Simplicity

- Critics argue that the Minimalist Program's assertion of simplicity could be misleading.
- Despite the reduction of core principles in MP, concepts such as phases, Agree, and feature checking introduce new layers of abstraction.
- Paul Postal and Geoffrey Pullum have expressed their dissatisfaction with MP's opaqueness and inaccessibility, stating that it complicates rather than simplifies the study of language.

8. Issues with Interface Conditions (LF and PF)

- Critics claim that the Minimalist Program's assumption of syntactic structures being compatible with Logical Form (LF) and Phonological Form (PF) simplifies the complex interplay between syntax and other language components.
- According to Ray Jackendoff, MP fails to comprehend the full complexity of the syntax-semantics and syntax-phonology interfaces. The Parallel Architecture model he advocates for proposes a more integrated view of language, where syntax, semantics, and phonology work in parallel instead of through a derivational process.

Important Critics of the Minimalist Program

1. Paul Postal expressed dissatisfaction with MP's lack of empirical rigor and its tendency to redefine problems rather than solve them.

2. Geoffrey Sampson questions the innateness of UG and the empirical basis of MP.
3. According to Ray Jackendoff, MP is oversimplified in terms of syntax, semantics, and phonology.
4. Michael Tomasello advocated for a language that is based on usage, with a focus on social and cognitive factors.
5. Philip Lieberman questioned the biological validity of MP's claims regarding the language faculty.
6. Through his work on Piraha, Daniel Everett gave examples that oppose recursion, which is one of the key aspects of Chomsky's UG
7. MP neglects the diversity of language(s) in use and their functional aspects, as described by Nicholas Evans and Stephen Levinson.

The Minimalist Program has provided key insights into how syntax and the human language faculty function. However, it has faced bitter resistance from linguists who dispute its basic assumptions, its methods and its universality. While such MP's intent is to show how simple and elegant language can be, critics say it often misses the bigger picture of our linguistic diversity, functional considerations and the complex interplay of language and cognition. Such criticisms illustrate the need for a more multifaceted approach to understanding the human ability to use language. The demand for an increasingly inclusive interpretation should motivate and inspire all linguists, cognitive researchers, and students of language principles to take part in the current talk and broaden our comprehension.

Chomsky's Replies to Critics of the Minimalist Program (MP)

- Critiques of the Minimalist Program (MP) have been addressed by Noam Chomsky himself in several writings, interviews, and lectures, and there is no doubt that these critiques have been raised by many who have been concerned about its assumptions, empirical basis, and conceptual framework, to name but some issues. Here's a recap of how he responds to major attacks:

On the Abstract Nature of MP and Its Empirical Testability

1. On the Objection, MP is too abstract, too abstract to be subject to empirical tests.

- Chomsky's Reply:
- Chomsky says MP's abstractness is required for scientific investigation, not a defect. When it comes to linguistics and other sciences like physics, which often use abstract models of the world that can't be directly observed, he finds that people often confuse the theoretical with the real (e.g., quantum mechanics).
- He proposes that MP is to uncover the fundamental principles of the language faculty (UG) and is thus more focused on explanatory adequacy than descriptive adequacy.
- He stresses that linguistic theory is not about cataloguing surface variation but rather about discovering the universal principles that produce it.

2. On the "Idealization" of Language Faculty

Criticism: MP idealises the language faculty as "optimal," ignoring real-world irregularities and redundancies.

Chomsky's Reply:

- According to Chomsky, the optimality assumption is only an experimental tool, not a concrete claim. Its purpose is to investigate the possibility that the language faculty operates efficiently in its core design, even if external factors (e.g., performance, historical evolution) cause irregularities.
- He distinguishes between competence (the idealized understanding of language) and performance (the actual usage of language), arguing that MP focuses on competence to comprehend the internal workings of language.

3. On Linguistic Diversity and Universality

Criticism: MP ignores linguistic diversity and is biased towards a few well-studied languages.

Chomsky's Reply:

- According to Chomsky, linguistic diversity is caused by externalization processes instead of the language's core computational system (such as phonological and morphological variation).
- The aim of MP is to explain the universal properties of syntax, not the surface-level differences between languages. According to him, the primary cause of these differences is the interaction with external systems such as sensory-motor systems and historical changes.
- He acknowledges the importance of cross-linguistic data, but insists that it should be interpreted according to more fundamental universal principles.

4. On Evolution and Biological Plausibility

Criticism: MP's view of language as an optimal and innate system lacks biological and evolutionary plausibility.

Chomsky's Reply:

- Chomsky believes that a single evolutionary mutation could have caused the language faculty to emerge, which in turn led to the development of Merge as FL's defining feature.
- He claims that evolutionary accounts for the origins of language are speculative, though he stresses that MP focuses on the structural properties of language, and that he leaves biological origins to embodied inter-disciplinary investigation.
- He has pointed out that biological systems often have optimal behaviour in their interiors while permitting defects on the outside, just like the language faculty.

5. On the Role of Social and Functional factors

Critique: He blinds himself to social, cognitive and functional factors in language.

Chomsky's Reply:

- Although it is accepted that language use pertains to social interaction and interacts with other cognitive systems, the core syntactic system (UG) is also maintained to be independent of these (Chomsky 1991).
- His argument is that social interaction or other external influences can shape the use of language but not its underlying rules.

6. On Vagueness in Concepts like Merge, Agree, and Phases

Criticism: Key concepts in MP are underdefined, leading to theoretical flexibility.

Chomsky's Reply.

- Chomsky has noted MP as a framework that is always in the process of community innovation. Elements like Merge, Agree, and phases are constantly being upgraded because of new data and theoretical developments.
- According to him, MP's ability to flexibly adapt to empirical discoveries without sacrificing core principles is a great strength.
- He has argued for the simplicity of these principles, maintaining that their abstract nature manifests their role as primitive operations of the language faculty.

7. On Piraha and the Universality of Recursion

Criticism: Studies like Daniel Everett's on Piraha challenge the universality of recursion, a cornerstone of MP.

Chomsky's Reply:

- To be fair, though, some colleagues like Robert Berwick have claimed that recursion is a core component of the mathematical object of computation we know as the language system, even though it might not appear in some actual languages, such as Piraha.
- Recursion is thereby undetermined in the surface structure. Yet, the raw data into which our mental grammar is projected is recursive, which does not negate the non-negation of recursion in the underlying mental grammar.

- He has challenged the validity of certain empirical claims regarding Piraha, suggesting that they could have been misinterpreted or affected by outside cultural factors.

8. On the Relation to Earlier Frameworks

Criticism: MP is a repackaging of earlier theories with new terminology.

Chomsky's Reply:

- Chomsky, however, considers MP a natural advancement of previous frameworks, sharpening and streamlining the insights that such frameworks laid out.
- GB theory introduced modular constraints, but MP focuses on replacing those constraints with what can be shown from a smaller set of principles. Therefore, MP can be a more elegant and explanatory theory

Chomsky's response to MP critics demonstrates his commitment to uncovering the fundamental properties of the language faculty by abstracting, idealising, and simplifying. He acknowledges MP's shortcomings but views them as a part of the natural process of scientific advancement. Chomsky explains that MP requires ongoing development and collaboration with other disciplines. Still, it provides a deeper and more principled understanding of human language by focusing on the core computational system.

Minimalism Today And Tomorrow

The Minimalist Program (MP) is a significant development in generative grammar because it offers a streamlined and theoretically elegant approach to understanding the human language faculty. MP aims to uncover the essential mechanisms underlying language by simplifying linguistic theory to its most fundamental principles, such as Merge and economic conditions, and emphasising efficiency and simplicity in its design. Building on earlier frameworks like Government and Binding (GB) Theory, MP consolidates previous insights while introducing a deeper focus on the interfaces between syntax, semantics, and phonology, bridging linguistic theory with broader cognitive processes.

MP's potential extends far beyond the realm of theoretical syntax. Its focus on identifying universal principles makes it a powerful tool for comparative linguistics, enabling researchers to examine cross-linguistic variation in a unified framework. In addition, MP's alignment with cognitive science principles demonstrates its importance in understanding the human mind. Furthermore, it is helpful in fields such as psychology, providing insights into the nature of human cognition and the unique abilities of the species. The idea of the language faculty has influenced research in neuroscience and artificial intelligence as an innate computational system, where MP principles are used in models of language processing and learning.

MP faces the dual challenge of refining its theoretical constructs and integrating empirical findings from diverse languages and cognitive domains in the future. Future research is expected to examine how MP can more effectively account for linguistic diversity, address criticisms of its idealised assumptions, and connect more effectively with functional and social aspects of language. MP is a framework that continually evolves, driving the generative enterprise towards a deeper understanding of language and positioning itself as a vital tool for both linguistic inquiry and interdisciplinary collaboration.

The Minimalist Program's contributions go beyond linguistic theory, revealing significant insights into the nature of human cognition and the shared design of the mind. This reinforces its importance as a cornerstone in language study and its place in human psychology and cognitive evolution.

CHAPTER VIII

EPILOGUE

We are on the verge of our journey through the intricacies of generative grammar. Though it was not an in-depth exploration of the grammatical system, we have certainly succeeded in becoming acquainted with its core philosophy and how it has evolved to the present day. We have witnessed many developments, rectifications, and even rewritings that have made the theories more scientific and promising. There is still room for more advancements as no scientific achievement is complete until it prompts a question.

Even the hardest critic will acknowledge that Noam Chomsky's contributions to linguistics and cognition are ground-breaking, scientific, and futuristic, and no study in this field can bypass them. From the beginning of the ideas of lexicon and phrase-structure rules, not only the thought process but also the evaluation process underwent a paradigm shift from behaviourist notations to the innateness of the human mind. For example, at the commencement of generative theories, the question was whether they were descriptive or prescriptive. Later, the issue was with the reasoning of descriptive adequacy, but at the point of minimalism, we saw a gradual shift towards explanatory adequacy.

The introduction of the concept of Language Faculty became one of the most thought-provoking questions during all these developments. Noam Chomsky asserted that men of science and rationality consider language's emergence, acquisition, and usage a branch of pure science, similar to physics, biology, or mathematics. He urged the scientific community to begin studying language with this perspective, starting with the alphabet, as everything up until now has been based on incorrect assumptions and guesswork.

Of course, these have impacted a wide range of fields, including psychology, philosophy, artificial intelligence, and computational language. Following the introduction of PSRs, he promoted the idea of universal grammar and the universality of language through every development, either adding or removing theories. The most recent version, the Minimalist Program (MP), is the result, and it is compact, elegant, and simple.

Language is for thought, not for communication.

Chomsky's argument that language is a tool for thought or projection of language as primarily a thought process led to a significant discussion among linguists and experts from different socio-scientific arenas. We are familiar with the idea, as per Chomsky, that I-language and E-language are the two parts of language, the first representing internalised language properties and the second representing externalised language properties. This will be helpful in understanding the crux of Chomsky's controversial language for thought remarks. By defining internalised language as the process of thinking and externalised language as communication, the controversy will be resolved. Naturally, the question arises of what prompted the debate if the matter is so simple. A short discussion may lead to some insights on this subject.

Language is a subject specific to the human species, but it is not a manmade phenomenon. It is a by-product of human evolution, meaning that, like many other cognitive and other capabilities, language emerged from the sheer necessity of human existence. This perspective should be used to view and measure everything related to language. Each function in humans has a primary organ to accomplish it, but each organ may have more than a single function. Language is also an exclusive function of an organ, even if it is not yet established. It is called the Language Faculty (LF), and its primary function is to express thought. The meaning of Chomsky's demand is that the intellectual world should start studying language from a basic level and avoid all guesswork.

He clarifies that language has a primary function of expression of thoughts and a secondary function of communication, such as locomotion being the primary function of legs and playing football being the secondary or tertiary function. Since language is the basis of thought, and both language and thoughts are restricted to humans, syntax is the means by which thoughts are formed. The Minimalist program, which is the most recent revision of syntax theory, brings simplicity, compactness, and naturalness to syntax. To conclude this discussion, Chomsky's understanding of language, regardless of any controversy, is a discovery that transforms entire debates on language, its origin, and usage.

Lexicon to Minimalism.

Since the beginning of Phrase Structure Rules (PSRs), generative grammar has been focused on language's universality and the theories that govern it. The theories underwent an evolutionary process to address this core issue and adapt to cross-linguistic variations. During each stage, new revolutionary frameworks emerged to tackle linguistic complexity and were refined in the following stage, either dropping the previous one or rectifying them. The deep structure and surface structure theory, which was the basis of transformational grammar, provides a dynamic interplay between form and meaning, maturing as LF and PF in MP. The universal binary branching of X-Bar theory, which resolved hierarchical structural issues, contributed to modularity, which was the basis for later versions of theories such as the Principles and Parameters theory and the Government and Binding theory. The principles and parameters theory asserts that language variations are universal and language-specific as a means to tackle cross-linguistic variations based on these theories. This paradigm shift enabled the systematic explanation of syntactic diversity while still maintaining a universal foundation. The Syntactic-sematic issues were addressed by the Government and Binding Theory by addressing the remaining structural and thematic relationships. When we reflect on this point of development, the structural pattern, tree diagram, and all related operations appear to be bulky, complex, and confusing. The Minimalist Programme emerged by stripping all these complexities to the minimum in terms of operations and content.

Cross-linguistic applicability of Minimalist Programme.

The economy of derivation and representation is one of the key concepts of the Minimalist Programme, which is achieved by performing core minimum operations such as Merge, Move, and Agree. The Minimalist Programme, as per Chomsky, employs these essential operations to make language structure universal. So, the empirical experiment with diverse languages worldwide is the only acceptable proof for this claim.

There are 7,000+ languages on all continents, with diametrically different features reflecting diverse cultures, social setups, and histories. Some classical languages, like Sanskrit and Latin, became extinct, and forty per cent of the existing languages are endangered. Some have billions of users, while some are limited to tens or hundreds. They can be found on mountaintops and remote islands, along with their inhabitants. The picture illustrates the difficulty of conducting a cross-linguistic case study throughout the world.

Over the past three decades, extensive empirical studies on different dimensions of theories have yielded mixed reactions, with both successes and challenges. The Minimalist Programme's partial success in cross-linguistic analytical studies raises many questions about its universality and how it will address it. An extensive research effort is being made to address the issues by refining the UG principles and simultaneously addressing criticisms about over-abstraction and Eurocentrism. The subject of falsification or verification depends on various factors that exist in the current scenario. However, the issues raised by Generative Grammar and the theories formed consequently would be the most relevant to this field.

Anarchism and Minimalism

It is interesting to draw anomalies or similarities between the minimalist program, a linguistic theory, and Anarchism, a political ideology, as both are inseparably related to Noam Chomsky. Anarchism, also known as libertarian socialism, is a political philosophy that advocates for a society run amicably on the innate tendencies of human beings with nil or minimal interference from the state. The Minimalist Programme, as we have gone through, is a linguistic theory with minimal structure and operations that is based on innate mental grammar.

On several occasions, Noam Chomsky stated that both interests are different and should not be compared or contrasted. Even though there is no direct link between political philosophy and linguistic theory, we will see certain connections, at least as far as Chomsky's approaches are concerned. The primary focus is on the innate characteristics of humans as a species, which they acquire through an evolutionary process. Man is the man, as his language and cognition developed to a level that no other species on earth could. Free will, freedom, and collectiveness may be the basis of society; therefore, the interference of the state or any similar mechanism will be disastrous and devastating for society. In other words, any sort of instruction is external and so resisted. Similarly, the acquisition, usage, and grammar of language depend on spontaneity, not on teaching or any prescribed methods. In both cases, Chomsky is against hierarchical structures and stands for naturality and simplicity.

The important difference to mention here is that the minimalist programme is developed using a scientific approach, which can be falsified or verified, however, anarchism remains an abstract idea that cannot be proven. Anarchism is based on a moral philosophy extracted from the history and nature of present-day states, especially that of the US aligned to imperialism. In contrast, the minimalist programme relies on formal modelling, empirical data, and cognitive science.

This book's subject matter does not relate to the parallels or conflicts drawn here. On the other hand, it was an interesting question that was genuinely raised in everyone's mind because Chomsky is a towering intellectual who is committed to both.

Conclusion

Although our book began as an introductory discussion on Generative Grammar, of course, based on Noam Chomsky's legacy, it raises several questions about language in its final phase: its origin, acquisition, usage, and cognition. Even terms otherwise defined in a simple way, such as language and grammar, become much more complicated or need to be read contextually. If this book stirs the reader's mind to prompt such numerous questions, the purpose of this book has been met. Regardless, the pursuit of universal principles, the primary pillar of generative grammar, has forever changed how we understand the connection between language, thought, and creativity. Furthermore, we understand that the continuation of the study on the topic requires more interdisciplinary research, which could lead to unexplored areas of linguistics study.

BIBLIOGRAPHY

Chomsky, Noam. Syntactic Structures. The Hague: Mouton, 1957.

Chomsky, Noam. Aspects of the Theory of Syntax. Cambridge, MA: MIT Press, 1965.

Chomsky, Noam. Lectures on Government and Binding: The Pisa Lectures. Dordrecht: Foris Publications, 1981.

Chomsky, Noam. The Minimalist Program. Cambridge, MA: MIT Press, 1995.

Jackendoff, Ray. Semantics and Cognition. Cambridge, MA: MIT Press, 1983.

Jackendoff, Ray. Foundations of Language: Brain, Meaning, Grammar, Evolution. Oxford: Oxford University Press, 2002.

Postal, Paul. On Raising: One Rule of English Grammar and Its Theoretical Implications. Cambridge, MA: MIT Press, 1974.

Lakoff, George. Generative Semantics: Studies in Language. The Hague: Mouton, 1971.

Lakoff, George, and Mark Johnson. Metaphors We Live By—Chicago: University of Chicago Press, 1980.

Joshi, Aravind K. Tree Adjoining Grammars: How Much Context-Sensitivity is Required to Provide Reasonable Structural Descriptions? Cambridge, MA: MIT Press, 1987.

Joshi, Aravind K., and Yves Schabes. Tree-Adjoining Grammars. In Handbook of Formal Languages, edited by G. Rozenberg and A. Salomaa, 69-123. Berlin: Springer, 1997.

Ross, John Robert. Constraints on Variables in Syntax. PhD diss., MIT, 1967.

Harman, Gilbert. Deep Structure as Logical Form. Synthese, 21(3-4), 275-297, 1970.

Parsons, Terence. Events in the Semantics of English: A Study in Subatomic Semantics. Cambridge, MA: MIT Press, 1990.

Carnie, Andrew. Syntax: A Generative Introduction. 4th ed. Hoboken, NJ: Wiley-Blackwell, 2021.

Cook, Vivian J., and Mark Newson. Chomsky's Universal Grammar: An Introduction. 3rd ed. Oxford: Wiley-Blackwell, 2007.

Lasnik, Howard, and Juan Uriagereka. A Course in GB Syntax: Lectures on Binding and Empty Categories. Cambridge, MA: MIT Press, 1988.

Smith, Neil. Chomsky: Ideas and Ideals. 3rd ed. Cambridge: Cambridge University Press, 2004.

Hornstein, Norbert, Jairo Nunes, and Kleanthes K. Grohmann. Understanding Minimalism. Cambridge: Cambridge University Press, 2005.

Syntactic Islands, Cedric Boeckx, Cambridge University Press. 2012

An Integrated Transformational Grammar of the English Language. Garland Cannon, Texas A&M University. 1978

On language, Penguin Random House, India, Pvt. Ltd. 2003

The Essential Chomsky, Edited by Antony Arnove, the Bodley Head London. 2008.

Phrase Structure Composition and Syntactic Dependencies, Robert Frank, MIT Press, Cambridge. 2002

Generative Grammar, Theory and Its History, Robert Fredin, Routledge. 2007.

Malayalam Verbs, Walter de Gruyter.

The Syntax Construction Kit, Mark Rosenfelder, Yonagu Books 2018

Parameters and Universals, Richard S Kayne, oxford Studies In Comparative Syntax, university Press, 2000.

Evolution of Chomsky's Transformational Grammar, EL Mouatamid Ben Rochd

Syntactic Islands, Cedric Boeckx, Cambridge University Press, 2012.

An Integrated Transformational Grammar of the English Language, Garland Cannon, A&M University, 1978.

Chomsky's Minimalism, Pieter A.M. Seuren, Oxford University Press, 2004.

Lectures on Language as Particularly Connected with English Grammar, William Stevens Balch, Providence B. Cranston &co,

Basic English Syntax, Mark Newson, Bolcsesz Konsorcium, 2006

NOAM CHOMSKY

Noam Chomsky, born on December 7, 1928, in Philadelphia, Pennsylvania, is a towering figure in linguistics, philosophy, cognitive science, and political activism. He revolutionised the study of language with his groundbreaking theory of generative grammar, introduced in Syntactic Structures (1957). This theory proposed that all human languages share a deep structural similarity, rooted in what he termed Universal Grammar, fundamentally altering the understanding of language acquisition and cognitive processes. His later works, such as Aspects of the Theory of Syntax (1965)

and The Minimalist Program (1995), continued to shape modern linguistic theory.

In addition to his linguistic achievements, Chomsky is a prominent critic of U.S. foreign policy and a staunch advocate for social justice. His political ideas emphasise anti-imperialism, opposition to corporate power, and the necessity of grassroots activism. Notable works in this realm include Manufacturing Consent (co-authored with Edward S. Herman, 1988), which critiques media manipulation and propaganda, and Hegemony or Survival (2003), where he explores U.S. global dominance. Chomsky has authored over 100 books, making significant contributions across multiple disciplines, and remains an influential voice in both academic and political spheres.

ABOUT THE AUTHOR

M.M. Sasi

M.M. Sasi, born in Kerala in 1956, is an educator, linguist, and writer who has dedicated his life to learning and social transformation. In his youth, he actively participated in theatre, the library movement, literacy education, the science movement, and political activism, laying the foundation for his lifelong commitment to education and community development.

Later, Sasi moved to Telangana, where, with the steadfast support of his life companion, Mrs. K.P. Annie, he founded the Good Morning Educational Society. Together, they established schools in remote villages, bringing education to marginalised communities. His interest in innovative teaching methods led him to adopt Montessori education, and he later published Montessori: A Brief Guide, a practical resource on this educational philosophy.

As an English teacher for decades, Sasi inspired countless students with his love for language and learning. While he initially recognised Noam Chomsky as a political commentator, activist, and philosopher, it was through the widespread availability of the internet that he became acquainted with Chomsky's linguistic theories. Intrigued by the concept of generative grammar, Sasi immersed himself in studying Chomsky's work and linguistic philosophy.

Observing a gap in concise and accessible resources on the topic, Sasi took on the challenge of writing his book, resulting in Generative Grammar (Chomskyan or Universal): An Introductory Handbook. This work serves as an approachable introduction to Chomsky's linguistic ideas, crafted to make the subject understandable to readers new to the field.

M.M. Sasi's journey—from his early activism in Kerala to his transformative work in education in Telangana and his contribution to linguistics—reflects his enduring passion for knowledge, teaching, and empowering others.

www.ingramcontent.com/pod-product-compliance
Ingram Content Group UK Ltd.
Pitfield, Milton Keynes, MK11 3LW, UK
UKHW062310290726
14090UKWH00018B/993